Matrix
Computing for 11–14

Teacher Handbook

Alison Page
Howard Lincoln
Diane Levine

Great Clarendon Street, Oxford, OX2 6DP, United Kingdom

Oxford University Press is a department of the University of Oxford. It furthers the University's objective of excellence in research, scholarship, and education by publishing worldwide. Oxford is a registered trade mark of Oxford University Press in the UK and in certain other countries

British Library Cataloguing in Publication Data
Data available

9780198395577

1 3 5 7 9 10 8 6 4 2

Paper used in the production of this book is a natural, recyclable product made from wood grown in sustainable forests. The manufacturing process conforms to the environmental regulations of the country of origin.

Printed in Great Britain

Acknowledgements
Cover illustration: Koivo at Good Illustration

Although we have made every effort to trace and contact all copyright holders before publication this has not been possible in all cases. If notified, the publisher will rectify any errors or omissions at the earliest opportunity.
Links to third party websites are provided by Oxford in good faith and for information only. Oxford disclaims any responsibility for the materials contained in any third party website referenced in this work.

Contents

Introduction

The *Matrix* series prepares students for the digital world through a real-life, project-based approach.

This handbook accompanies the first Student Book in the *Matrix* series. There are three books in the *Matrix Computing for 11–14* series, *Matrix 1* (Year 7), *Matrix 2* (Year 8) and *Matrix 3* (Year 9). The books combine to meet the Computing Programme of Study (age 11–14) for England. They also combine to meet the Computing at School (CAS) objectives for secondary students. Each chapter will help you to teach a six-week block of lessons of computer science.

English as an additional language

The *Matrix* series is written clearly for students and teachers with English as an additional language. Writers have used short sentences with a strong focus. They have avoided long sentences and unnecessary words that could get in the way of a reader's understanding.

Lessons identify and define key words that are central to the topic and may be new to students. These key words are highlighted and defined when they first appear in the lesson. Key words appear again, with their definitions, at the end of the lesson in a Key words box.

This handbook offers a language development section designed to help with any potentially new or useful language associated with that lesson. This is particularly useful when specific word or phrase may have a different technical meaning from its use in everyday English. This section explains the difference in meanings and encourages you to explore these words with students.

Structure of each Student Book in the *Matrix* series

All three Student Books have a consistent design and structure. Each book is divided into six chapters.

1 Computational Thinking: Apply logical problem-solving approaches to real-life problems.
2 App Inventor: Create working apps for mobile phones and tablets using a visual programming language.
3 Data and the CPU: Learn the basics of binary maths and the electronics that make a computer processor work.
4 Introducing Python: Use a high-level programming language used by professional programmers.
5 Information Technology: Discover the hardware and software that make up a computer system. Learn to use these safely and responsibly.
6 Creative Communication: Use technology to create a website, conduct research, design and analyse survey data.

Each chapter in the Student Book contains the following.

↗ **Introductory pages:** The first two chapter pages introduce the topic and show students what they will learn. These pages are designed to help you engage students. They offer ideas for an activity you can do, or discussion you can have, without a computer. A Word cloud shows all the key words that are defined in each lesson throughout the chapter.

↗ **Six lessons:** Each four-page lesson in the Student Book starts by highlighting what students will do during that lesson. The lesson is divided into sections that provide knowledge and skills development. A learning activity, an extension activity and a differentiated short test of four or five questions helps you check students' understanding. Each lesson is divided into these sections:

  ○ ⌘ **Learn about... :** Sets out the facts that students need to know before they complete the exercise and activities that follow.

  ○ ⏻ **How to... :** Guides students through a practical exercise, building their understanding of the lesson topic.

- o ⊕ **Learning activity:** Offers one or more independent activities students can complete, once they have finished the earlier sections. These activities are an opportunity for students to reflect on the learning objectives of the lesson.

- o 🌐 **If you have time... :** This extension activity stretches and challenges more-able students.

- o 📄 **Test yourself... :** Four or five short questions give students an opportunity to review what they have learned and make sure they have understood the topic.

↗ **Key words:** The key words from each lesson appear in the Word cloud in the chapter's introductory pages. The Word cloud introduces these new words to students. Key words are shown in bold when they are first introduced in the lessons. They are also summarised in a Key words box at the end of most lessons. The key words in the lessons reinforce learning.

↗ **Fact:** Many chapters will highlight a fact about the lesson topic to encourage students' interest.

↗ **Review:** The end-of-chapter review contains:

- o 📑 **Test questions:** Ten test questions give students an opportunity to reflect on what they have learned.

- o ✅ **Assessment activities:** There are three levels of differentiated assessment activities—starter, intermediate and extension.

Structure of each Teacher Handbook in the *Matrix* series

Each Teacher Handbook in the *Matrix* series follows the structure of the corresponding Student Book, offering guidance to plan and deliver the Student Book lessons.

Introduction

The introduction to this handbook:

↗ explains the Student Book and the Teacher Handbook structures

↗ highlights the Computing Programme of Study (age 11–14) for England objectives addressed in the Student Books

↗ identifies the CAS objectives addressed in the Student Books

↗ shows what students will do in the *Matrix 1* Student Book, along with the corresponding curriculum objectives

↗ offers details on the programming languages App Inventor and Python, and how to install the software

↗ suggests the ways you can differentiate classroom work according to students' ability and English language experience.

Two-page chapter introduction

↗ **Curriculum coverage:** Lists the Computing Programme of Study (age 11–14) for England objectives and CAS objectives for that chapter.

↗ **Preparation**: Explains what you need to do before starting work on the chapter with students.

↗ **Learning outcomes:** Show what students will achieve during the chapter.

↗ **Introductory pages:** Offer ideas for discussion topics and activities based on the corresponding section in the Student Book.

↗ **Six lesson guides:**

- o **Overview**: Explains what students will do in the chapter.

- o **Language development:** Highlights words that have a different technical meaning to their everyday English language use and any other important language issues.

- o **Before the lesson**: Identifies the preparation you will need to make the lesson a success. This section also highlights the key words from the lesson which you may want to review yourself, ahead of time.

- o ⌘ **Learn about... :** Explains how you will lead this part of the lesson and outlines the ideas that students must understand before moving on to the next part of the lesson.

- ⏻ **How to... :** Shows how you can guide students through an exercise, which they will complete.

- ⊕ **Learning activity:** Provides model answers to questions or examples of what success looks like if students have correctly completed the activity.

- 🌐 **If you have time... :** Gives examples of what success looks like if students have correctly completed the extension activity.

- ▤ **Test yourself... :** Offers model answers to the four or five short test questions to help you assess students' learning. Where more than one answer is possible, the handbook suggests several possible correct answers. You can set these questions as homework or they can be done in class.

Review

The end-of-chapter review contains the following.

↗ ▣ **Model answers to test questions:** Ten test questions give students an opportunity to reflect on what they have learned. This handbook provides correct answers to the test questions. Where more than one answer is possible, the handbook suggests several possible correct answers.

↗ ✓ **Model answers to assessment activities:** There are three levels of differentiated assessment activities—starter, intermediate and extension. This handbook provides examples of successful approaches to each activity. Where more than one approach is possible, the handbook suggests more than one approach.

Meeting the Computing Programme of Study (age 11–14) for England objectives

By age 14, students in England are expected to know, apply and understand the matters, skills and processes specified in the relevant programme of study. The table lists each skill for computing and shows where the *Matrix* series covers each Computing Programme of Study objective.

Computing Programme of Study for England	Book 1	Book 2	Book 3
Design, use and evaluate computational abstractions that model the state and behaviour of real-world problems and physical systems.	Ch 1	Ch 1	Ch 1
Understand several key algorithms that reflect computational thinking.	Ch 1	Ch 1	Ch 1
Understand algorithms for sorting and searching.		Ch 1	Ch 1
Use logical reasoning to compare the utility of alternative algorithms for the same problem.			Ch 1
Use two or more programming languages, at least one of which is textual, to solve a variety of computational problems.	Ch 2, 4	Ch 2, 4	Ch 2, 4
Make appropriate use of data structures [for example, lists, tables or arrays].		Ch 4	Ch 4
Design and develop modular programs that use procedures or functions.			Ch 2.4
Understand simple Boolean logic [for example, AND, OR and NOT] and some of its uses in circuits and programming.		Ch 3, 4	Ch 3, 4
Understand how numbers can be represented in binary.	Ch 3	Ch 3	
Carry out simple operations on binary numbers [for example, binary addition, and conversion between binary and decimal].	Ch 3	Ch 3	
Understand the hardware and software components that make up computer systems, and how they communicate with one another and with other systems.	Ch 5	Ch 5	Ch 5
Understand how instructions are stored and executed within a computer system; understand how data of various types (including text, sounds and pictures) can be represented and manipulated digitally, in the form of binary digits.			Ch 3, 5
Undertake creative projects that involve selecting, using, and combining multiple applications, preferably across a range of devices, to achieve challenging goals, including collecting and analysing data and meeting the needs of known users.	Ch 6	Ch 6	Ch 6
Create, re-use, revise and re-purpose digital artefacts for a given audience, with attention to trustworthiness, design and usability.	Ch 2, 4, 6	Ch 2, 4, 6	Ch 2, 4, 6
Understand a range of ways to use technology safely, respectfully, responsibly and securely, including protecting their online identity and privacy; recognise inappropriate content, contact and conduct, and know how to report concerns.	Ch 5	Ch 5	Ch 5

CAS Progression Pathways

Computing At School (CAS) provides guidance for computing teachers and has developed pathway objectives for computing at primary and secondary levels. These are the CAS Progression Pathways objectives covered in the *Matrix* series:

Purple objectives	Matrix books (M)
Algorithms	
Understands that iteration is the repetition of a process such as a loop.	Ch 1, 4 (M 1, 2, 3)
Recognises that different algorithms exist for the same problem.	Ch 1 (M 2, 3)
Represents solutions using a structured notation.	Ch 1 (M 1, 2, 3); Ch 4 (M 1)
Can identify similarities and differences in situations and can use these to solve problems (pattern recognition).	Ch 1 (M 1, 2, 3)
Programming & Development	
Understands that programming bridges the gap between algorithmic solutions and computers.	Ch 1 (M 1, 2, 3); Ch 2, Ch 4 (M 1)
Has practical experience of a high-level textual language, including using standard libraries when programming.	Ch 4 (M 1, 2, 3)
Uses a range of operators and expressions e.g. Boolean, and applies them in the context of program control.	Ch 2, 4 (M 1, 2, 3)
Selects the appropriate data types.	Ch 2, Ch 4 (M 1, 2, 3)
Data & Data Representation	
Knows that digital computers use binary to represent all data.	Ch 3 (M 1, 2, 3)
Understands how bit patterns represent numbers and images.	Ch 3 (M 1, 2, 3)
Knows that computers transfer data in binary.	Ch 3 (M 1, 2, 3)
Understands the relationship between binary and file size (uncompressed).	Ch 3 (M 2)
Defines data types: real numbers and Boolean.	Ch 2, Ch 4 (M2)
Hardware & Processing	
Recognises and understands the function of the main internal parts of basic computer architecture.	Ch 3 (M 3)
Understands the concepts behind the fetch-execute cycle.	Ch 3 (M 3)
Knows that there is a range of operating systems and application software for the same hardware.	Ch 5 (M 1)
Communication & Networks	
Understands how search engines rank search results.	Ch 5 (M 2)
Understands how to construct static web pages using HTML and CSS.	Ch 6 (M 2)
Understands data transmission between digital computers over networks, including the Internet i.e. IP addresses and packet switching.	Ch 5 (M 2)
Information Technology	
Evaluates the appropriateness of digital devices, Internet services and application software to achieve given goals.	Ch 6 (M 1)
Recognises ethical issues surrounding the application of information technology beyond school.	Ch 6 (M 3)
Designs criteria to critically evaluate the quality of solutions, uses the criteria to identify improvements and can make appropriate refinements to the solution.	Ch 1, 2, 6 (M 1)
Red objectives	Matrix books (M)
Algorithms	
Recognises that some problems share the same characteristics and use the same algorithm to solve both.	Ch 1 (M 2)
Understands the notion of performance for algorithms and appreciates that some algorithms have different performance characteristics for the same task.	Ch 1 (M 1, 2, 3)
Programming & Development	
Uses nested selection statements.	Ch 2 (M 3); Ch 4 (M 2)
Appreciates the need for, and writes, custom functions including use of parameters.	Ch 2, 4 (M 3)
Knows the difference between, and uses appropriately, procedures and functions.	Ch 2, 4 (M 3)
Understands and uses negation with operators.	Ch 2 (M 3)
Uses and manipulates one-dimensional data structures.	Ch 4 (M 2, 3)
Detects and corrects syntactical errors.	Ch 2, 4 (M 1, 2, 3)
Data & Data Representation	
Understands how numbers, images, sounds and character sets use the same bit patterns.	Ch 3, (M 2, 3); Ch 5 (M 3)
Performs simple operations using bit patterns e.g. binary addition.	Ch 3 (M 2)

Understands the relationship between resolution and colour depth, including the effect on file size.	Ch 5 (M 3)
Distinguishes between data used in a simple program (a variable) and the storage structure for that data.	Ch 3 (M 2)
Hardware & Processing	
Understands the von Neumann architecture in relation to the fetch-execute cycle, including how data is stored in memory.	Ch 3 (M 3)
Understands the basic function and operation of location addressable memory.	Ch 3 (M 3)
Communication & Networks	
Knows the names of hardware e.g. hubs, routers, switches, and the names of protocols e.g. SMTP, IMAP, POP, FTP, TCP/IP, associated with networking computer systems.	Ch 5 (M 1, 2)
Uses technologies and online services securely, and knows how to identify and report inappropriate conduct.	Ch 5 (M 1, 2); Ch 6 (M 3)
Information Technology	
Evaluates the trustworthiness of digital content and considers the usability of visual design features when designing and creating digital artefacts for a known audience.	Ch 6 (M 3)
Identifies and explains how the use of technology can impact on society.	Ch 6 (M 3)
Designs criteria for users to evaluate the quality of solutions, uses the feedback from the users to identify improvements and can make appropriate refinements to the solution.	Ch 6 (M 3)
Black objectives	**Matrix books (M)**
Algorithms	
Recognises that the design of an algorithm is distinct from its expression in a programming language (which will depend on the programming constructs available).	Ch 1 (M 2, 3); Ch 4 (M 1, 2, 3)
Evaluates the effectiveness of algorithms and models for similar problems.	Ch 1 (M 1, 2, 3)
Recognises where information can be filtered out in generalising problem solutions.	Ch 1 (M 1, 2, 3)
Uses logical reasoning to explain how an algorithm works.	Ch 1 (M 1, 2, 3)
Represents algorithms using structured language.	Ch 1 (M 1, 2, 3)
Programming & Development	
Appreciates the effect of the scope of a variable e.g. a local variable can't be accessed from outside its function.	Ch 4 (M 3)
Understands and applies parameter passing.	Ch 4 (M 3)
Understands the difference between, and uses, both pre-tested e.g. 'while', and post-tested e.g. 'until' loops.	Ch 4 (M 2, 3) Ch 1 (M 2)
Applies a modular approach to error detection and correction.	Ch 4 (M 3)
Data & Data Representation	
Knows the relationship between data representation and data quality.	Ch 5 (M 3)
Understands the relationship between binary and electrical circuits, including Boolean logic.	Ch 3 (M 2, 3)
Understands how and why values are data typed in many different languages when manipulated within programs.	Ch 4 (M 3)
Hardware & Processing	
Knows that processors have instruction sets and that these relate to low-level instructions carried out by a computer.	Ch 3 (M 3)
Communication & Networks	
Knows the purpose of the hardware and protocols associated with networking computer systems.	Ch 5 (M 2, 3)
Understands the client-server model including how dynamic web pages use server-side scripting and that web servers process and store data entered by users.	Ch 5 (M 3)
Recognises that persistence of data on the Internet requires careful protection of online identity and privacy.	Ch 5 (M 2, 3)
Information Technology	
Undertakes creative projects that collect, analyse, and evaluate data to meet the needs of a known user group.	Ch 6 (M 1,2, 3)
Effectively designs and creates digital artefacts for a wider or remote audience.	Ch 2, 4, 6 (M 1, 2, 3)
Considers the properties of media when importing them into digital artefacts.	Ch 2 (M 1); Ch 6 (M 2); Ch 5 (M 3)
Documents user feedback, the improvements identified and the refinements made to the solution.	Ch 6 (M 3)
Explains and justifies how the use of technology impacts on society, from the perspective of social, economical, political, legal, ethical and moral issues.	Ch 6 (M 3)

What students will do in each chapter of *Matrix 1*

Chapter 1: Computational Thinking	
Students learn basic principles of computational thinking and use them to design a simple spam filter.	
Computing POS	Design, use and evaluate computational abstractions that model the state and behaviour of real-world problems and physical systems; Understand several key algorithms that reflect computational thinking.
CAS	Represent solutions using a structured notation; Understand that iteration is the repetition of a process such as a loop; Recognise where information can be filtered out in generalising problem solutions.

Chapter 2: App Inventor	
Students create an electronic ID card that they can use on a mobile phone or other device.	
Computing POS	Use at least two programming languages to solve a variety of computational problems; Create digital artefacts for a given audience.
CAS	Understand that programming bridges the gap between algorithmic solutions and computers; Use a range of operators and expressions e.g. Boolean, and apply them in the context of program control; Detect and correct syntactical errors.

Chapter 3: Data and the CPU	
Students learn about binary numbers and how to convert numbers between binary and decimal. They explore how computers use codes to convert binary numbers into information that we can understand.	
Computing POS	Understand how numbers can be represented in binary, and be able to carry out simple operations on binary numbers [conversion between binary and decimal].
CAS	Know that digital computers use binary to represent all data; Know that computers transfer data in binary; Distinguish between data used in a simple program (a variable) and the storage structure for that data.

Chapter 4: Introducing Python	
Students write a computer quiz. After every question the computer will tell them if they got the answer right. The computer will show the score at the end of the quiz.	
Computing POS	Use at least 2 programming languages, one of which is textual, to solve a variety of computational problems; Create digital artefacts for a given audience; Extended learning: Understand simple Boolean logic [for example, AND, OR and NOT] and some of its uses in programming.
CAS	Understand that programming bridges the gap between algorithmic solutions and computers; Have practical experience of a high-level textual language; Use a range of operators and expressions e.g. Boolean, and apply them in the context of program control; Select the appropriate data types; Define data types: real numbers and Boolean; Detect and correct syntactical errors.

Chapter 5: Information Technology	
Students learn how hardware is used, and explore the differences between system and application software. They also learn how to stay safe online.	
Computing POS	Understand the hardware and software components that make up computer systems and how they communicate with each other; Understand a range of ways to use technology safely, respectfully, responsibly and securely.
CAS	Know that there is a range of operating systems and application software for the same hardware.

Chapter 6: Creative communication	
Students learn to use HTML tags to create a web page. They also use Microsoft Expression Web 4 to create a website of two or more pages.	
Computing POS	Undertake creative projects that involve selecting, using, and combining multiple applications, to achieve challenging goals; Create digital artefacts for a given audience, with attention to trustworthiness, design and usability.
CAS	Evaluate the appropriateness of digital devices, Internet services and application software to achieve given goals; Design criteria to critically evaluate the quality of solutions, uses the criteria to identify improvements and can make appropriate refinements to the solution. Extended learning: Understand how to construct static web pages using HTML and CSS.

Prepare the programming languages

Students will work with two different programming languages in *Matrix 1*:

↗ App Inventor.

↗ Python.

Preparing to use App Inventor

App Inventor is a lively, visual language that is used in classrooms all over the world. It is hosted by MIT (Massachusetts Institute of Technology). App Inventor is freely available for you and students to use in class or at home. No prior experience is needed to use App Inventor.

Key facts about App Inventor:

↗ **App Inventor is cloud-based**: You open App Inventor in your Internet browser. Your work is saved on a remote server—not on your own computer.

↗ **To log in to App Inventor you need to have a Google Account**: All users of Gmail, for example, can use their Gmail login. Google accounts are free to set up. Some students may already have Gmail logins. You may want to set up additional accounts for students in your class.

↗ **You can run completed programs on an Android device or an on-screen emulator**: You will need to have one or both of these set up so students can run their completed programs.

Choose the right browser

You work on App Inventor by connecting to the website with a browser. The App Inventor team recommend that you use Firefox or Google Chrome to connect to App Inventor. Internet Explorer is not recommended.

To create a Google account, visit:

`https://accounts.google.com/signup`

You may create a group of accounts for your school, or encourage each student to set up their own Google account. Make sure students remember their passwords.

↗ App Inventor website:

`http://appinventor.mit.edu/`

↗ The App Inventor software is available at this URL. You will find any programs you and students have made at this location.
`http://ai2.appinventor.mit.edu/`

↗ Getting Started page:

`http://appinventor.mit.edu/explore/get-started.html`

Use an Android device

Once they have made their apps, students can run them on any Android device, such as a mobile phone or tablet. Students can use their own phones. This is a lively and exciting way for students to see their work come to life on their phone. You may want to have two or three spare Android phones or tablets in the classroom for students who do not have Android phones.

To run your app on an Android phone, make sure that:

↗ your computer is connected to a wireless network

↗ the phone is connected to the same wireless network

↗ the App Inventor Companion is installed on the phone.

To find out more and download the App Inventor Companion:

`http://appinventor.mit.edu/explore/ai2/setup-device-wifi.html`

You can run any app you make from the project screen. Open the Connect menu and select AI Companion.

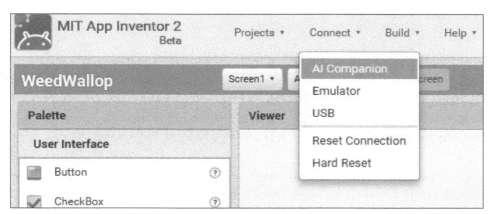

You will see a window like this.

The pattern is called a QR code. You can scan the QR code or enter the text code. The App should appear on the screen of your device.

Use the emulator

If you cannot use an Android device, the second best option is to use an emulator. The emulator looks like the screen of a mobile phone on your computer screen. You will see your app running on the screen. Many schools develop mainly on emulators and provide a few Android devices for final testing. You will have to install some software on your school computers called aiStarter.

Find out more about the emulator:

`http://appinventor.mit.edu/explore/ai2/setup-emulator.html`

If you are not sure whether to use the AI Companion or the emulator, discuss the options with your school technician or network administrator.

Further information

There is a variety of information on the App Inventor website.

- ↗ Support for teachers:
  `http://teach.appinventor.mit.edu/`
- ↗ Trouble-shooting connection issues:
  `http://appinventor.mit.edu/explore/ai2/connection-help.html`
- ↗ Full online documentation:
  `http://appinventor.mit.edu/explore/library.html`
- ↗ A document for school technicians, at the time of writing, is available at the following URL:
  `https://docs.google.com/document/d/1GMXO_GoCRj3052Pg93dzEzJ5sXido9Ul7Xrn6HYU6Xs/edit`

Make sure you test the App Inventor connection before you use it with students. Occasionally, organisational security settings, such as an Internet firewall, can interfere with the use of online services such as App Inventor. If you experience problems when you first use App Inventor, discuss this with your chief technician or head of IT.

Preparing to use Python

Python is a straightforward text-based programming language. Python can be downloaded for free and used on any computer without restriction. Go through the exercises and activities in the *Matrix* Student Book. In doing this, you will develop enough confidence and skills to lead students through the fundamentals of Python.

To download a copy of Python visit:

`https://www.python.org`

You will see links to the area of the site to download the files you need to write and run Python programs. At the time of writing the URL for this area was:

`https://www.python.org/downloads/`

You or your school or college technician can also use this link to download and install Python on all classroom computers.

Versions

More than one version of Python is available on the website. Python version numbers are constantly updated. However, differences between recent versions are minor, and it will not matter which version you use. Simply download the most up-to-date version available on the site.

Note: There are significant differences between versions of Python which begin with '2' (e.g. Python 2.3.1.) and those which begin with '3' (e.g. Python 3.4.4.). This book is written for any version of Python which begins with 3.

Differentiation and assessment of learning

The *Matrix* series focuses support for a range of students and includes supporting students who may struggle with challenging English-language content. This focus means that most students will achieve curriculum targets by working through the content of the books. It also means that confident and able students will be able to extend their understanding and demonstrate that understanding through extension activities and independent work.

You can assess students' progress by observing their completion of the learning activities (**Now you do it...**) for each lesson. The short test questions (**Test yourself...**) at the end of each lesson give you an additional opportunity to confirm progress and differentiate between students working at different levels. The test questions in each lesson are differentiated and colour-coded. The questions with the blue panel are for the Foundation level. The questions with the green panel are Extension questions.

In classes where most students have limited English, you may find that many fall into the 'needing support' category.

DEVELOPING UNDERSTANDING (students needing support): Some students may need several classroom sessions to complete a single lesson activity. These students may achieve only some of the goals set. This is better than rushing them to finish all set tasks without full understanding. Support students to complete as many learning activities as they can manage. Encourage students to at least complete the Foundation questions in the short test (**Test yourself...**) section.

SECURING UNDERSTANDING (most students): Most students will be able to follow the activities in each lesson, completing this work in one lesson, and answering the test questions that follow. The completion of practical work and answers to these questions will provide practical and written evidence of learning. Students with good English skills may be able to work from the guidance in the books. These students should successfully complete all Foundation questions and attempt Extension questions.

EXTENDING UNDERSTANDING (more-able students): Students who work with confidence will be able to complete activities working from the instruction in the book. They will have time to complete the extension activities (**If you have time...**) included with each lesson. Model answers to these activities are provided in the lesson guides that follow. Students should successfully complete the ten short test questions and the Starter to Extension activities in the review section at the end of the chapter. The extended test in the review section will give you the opportunity to check students' retention of skills and knowledge, and differentiate achievement. Practical activities at Starter, Intermediate and Extension level are included. Students should attempt as many of these as they can to show their understanding.

Summary of differentiation

	In a typical classroom session	Activities	Short tests	End-of-topic review
Students needing support or with language issues	May complete part of the content of one lesson.	May need help to complete the learning activity.	Will attempt the Foundation questions.	Will attempt the end-of-topic test. Will complete the Foundation activity.
Most students	Will cover the learning and skills content of one lesson.	Will complete the learning activity, working independently. May complete the Extension activity.	Will attempt all questions, getting all or most correct.	Will answer all questions in end-of-topic test. Will complete the Starter and Intermediate activities. If there is time, may attempt the Extension activity.
More-able students	Will cover all of one lesson including additional content linked to extension work. May move onto further lessons.	Will complete the main and Extension activities.	Will answer all questions correctly.	Will answer all questions correctly in the end-of-topic test. Will complete all activities.

1 Computational Thinking

Curriculum coverage

This chapter covers part or all of the requirements for the Computing Programme of Study (age 11–14):

↗ design, use and evaluate computational abstractions that model the state and behaviour of real-world problems and physical systems

↗ understand several key algorithms that reflect computational thinking.

This chapter also covers these main requirements for the Computing at School (CAS) Progression Pathways (for a full list of requirements met, see pages 9–10 of this handbook):

↗ understand that iteration is the repetition of a process such as a loop

↗ recognise where information can be filtered out in generalising problem solutions

↗ represent solutions using a structured notation.

Preparation

Computational thinking is a way to study computing and approach problem-solving in everyday life. Computational thinking helps students think through problems, break problems down into smaller parts and find good solutions. The foundations of computational thinking lie in logical reasoning. Logical reasoning is useful in many subjects, from science to history.

If you are teaching this topic for the first time, you may want to work through the student exercises before each lesson. You could also develop your own teaching examples to show students how they can apply computational thinking concepts to daily life in their own local context.

Games may be useful to help students learn the technical key words in this chapter. Create several sets of cards with individual key words on them. You can take these words from the Key words boxes in each lesson of the Student Book. Use all the terms for the year and play different word games as the year progresses. Only use words students understand for each lesson. Some suggestions for games are given in this handbook.

Learning outcomes

In this chapter students use computational thinking to solve the problem of designing a simple spam filter. First, students will learn to decompose the problem. Then they will find out how to recognise patterns when solving computing problems. Students will also discover how to represent problems using flowcharts and evaluate their solutions.

By completing this chapter students will be able to:

- describe computational thinking
- use decomposition to break a problem down into smaller parts
- describe an algorithm
- use pattern recognition
- use a flow chart to describe their problem-solving
- describe selection
- use `if... then... else` to navigate through a problem
- describe iteration
- use loops to navigate through a problem
- evaluate other people's work
- give helpful feedback.

Design a spam filter

Many of the activities in this chapter do not require a computer. Computational thinking is a way of thinking and solving problems. It can be represented with or without technology.

Offline activity

The introductory pages in the Student Book introduce the idea of computational thinking to students. Here is an extra offline activity that you can use to introduce computational thinking. You can use this task if the school computers are down, or if you need to work in a room with no computers. You will need: blindfolds, pieces of paper with one large coloured dot on each piece. Ask students to work in pairs or small groups. Give each group a colour. In each group, ask one student to cover his or her eyes or wear a blindfold. Now place the coloured dots around the room. Each group must give verbal instructions to the blindfolded student. The blindfolded student must find the coloured dot for their group. Ensure that obstacles such as chairs and bags are tidied away before you start.

Before you play the game ask students to think about:

- the problems they might face, for example, each group shouting instructions at the same time might be confusing for the blindfolded student
- ways of solving the problems
- the kinds of instructions that might be useful.

Talk about...

The discussion is also an activity you can do offline. You could use this activity any time to vary the pace of lessons and encourage students to reflect on their learning.

Discuss the blindfold game you have played. Support students in stating the problems they faced and the solutions they found.

Explain that computational thinking is a way of understanding and solving problems that can help us in computing and in our daily lives.

Ask students to discuss problems they encounter in their everyday lives. The Student Book gives two examples, but other examples you could discuss are:

- planning a meal
- preparing your clothes for a physical education lesson
- keeping in touch with family who live far away.

Choose a problem that interests students. Break the problem down into smaller parts. For example, the problem of keeping in touch with faraway family could include:

- whether you have access to a computer, or phone, and the Internet
- whether your faraway family have access to a computer or phone and the Internet
- whether there is a time difference between the two locations.

FACT

Seymour Papert was a computer scientist, mathematician and teacher. He was born in South Africa in 1928 and has lived and taught all over the world. His book *Mindstorms: Children, Computers and Powerful Ideas*, tells us that the ways children learn to use technology can make a difference to the ways they learn everything else.

`http://www.papert.org/`

Use this opportunity to ask students what they think about using computers to learn. Do computers help them learn? If so, how do computers help them to learn? Students might recall doing a quiz on a computer, or using the Internet to research a project. Encourage students to talk about the advantages of using computers for learning. Ask students if they can think of examples where computers might not be so helpful. Students might say that spending a lot of time on a computer could keep them from going outside and seeing their friends. Perhaps they enjoy listening to music or watching YouTube videos, which might also distract them from doing homework.

Word cloud

The Word cloud contains all the key words that have been highlighted and defined in Key words boxes throughout the lesson. The key words for this chapter are: process, computational thinking, spam filter, spam, algorithm, implement, loop, decomposition, flow chart, pattern recognition, sequencing, selection, iteration, variable, criteria, fit for purpose, efficient, elegant, data, command, sequence.

Learning outcomes

When they have completed this lesson students should be able to:

↗ describe computational thinking

↗ use decomposition to break a problem down into smaller parts.

More-confident students will:

↗ begin to identify and explain patterns.

Overview

This is the first lesson introducing computational thinking. Students do not need any prior learning in the subject. In this lesson students will find out more about what computational thinking is. Students learn why computational thinking is useful in computing and in everyday life. Students also apply computational thinking to the problem of designing a spam filter as their project for this chapter.

Language development

Students will discover that computational thinking is a way of thinking through problems and finding effective solutions. Students are also introduced to the term algorithm, which is a set of instructions or rules that we can follow to carry out a task.

The word 'decomposition' has a technical meaning in computational thinking. Decomposition means breaking down a problem into smaller parts. Based on your knowledge of students' language competencies, you may want to compare this meaning with a science-based meaning. For example, decomposition also refers to the process of organic matter decomposing in a composter.

Students are also introduced to the word 'spam'. Understanding that some emails are unsolicited and unwelcome is an important part of helping students keep safe online.

Before the lesson

You may want to set up an email account for the whole class. You could use this account to monitor incoming spam emails and discuss these, where appropriate, with students. Monitoring incoming spam emails would ensure that students base their understanding on real-life examples.

The key words for this lesson are: algorithm, computational thinking, decomposition, process, spam and spam filter. The words are highlighted when they first appear in the text. Their definitions are included in the Key words box at the end of the lesson. You may want to review these words before the lesson.

Learn about...

You will lead the first part of the lesson. Make sure students understand these ideas. You may ask them to make notes. You may use directed questioning to check understanding.

- **Algorithm:** An algorithm is a set of instructions or rules that we make to carry out a task or solve a problem.
- **Decomposition:** We use decomposition to break the problem down into smaller parts that are easier to solve.

How to...

In the second part of the lesson students complete an exercise under your guidance.

Look at the three smaller parts of the decomposed problem.

- What type of chocolate would sell well?
- How would you make it?
- How would you get it to customers?

Ask students to talk about whether the first decomposed problem is complete. The factory owners might also want to think about these points.

- Price: Is it important to think about how much money the factory would like to make first? How would this make a difference to the rest of the process?
- What ingredients can the factory use?
- Where will the chocolates be selling? What do people in those places like to eat?

Tell students that there are no right or wrong answers because context makes a big difference to any decomposition process. Decomposing a problem correctly means we need to think about the important factors in any particular context.

Read through the algorithms with students. Ask whether they agree with the algorithm given. Look at the task 'Find out what type of chocolate customers would like to buy'. The first line of the algorithm is 'Invent some chocolate ideas'.

Ask students if they think they could decompose the task further. They might suggest:

- bringing together a group of children to invent a new idea
- carrying out market research in a shop to find out what people would like.

⊕ Now you do it...

Students apply decomposition and algorithmic skills to the main project for this chapter, which is to design a simple email spam filter. Read through the text of this learning activity with students so they understand the idea of spam. Ask whether any of them have seen a spam email in real life. Explain that there are two ways to protect themselves from spam.

1 Learn to recognise spam in their email inboxes, and delete or report it if they see it.

2 Use an effective spam filter.

Students will work in pairs, using the two spam examples to answer the questions.

What success looks like:

- Who is the email from? Does the email match the email address? Answer: Example 1: Mrs Smith, this does not match the email address; Example 2: Honest Bank, this does match some of the email address but we would expect the email domain to be honestbank.com not cooltunes.com.
- Is the content of the email addressed to the email owner? Answer: Both examples: No.
- Does the email ask for personal details? Answer: Example 1: No; Example 2: Yes
- Does the email ask for money? Answer: Example 1: Yes; Example 2: No.
- What are the key words that your spam filter will detect? This is a more challenging question,

and students may need you to explain the meaning of 'key word' and 'detect'. Answer: A range of answers is possible, including: checking, account, bank, banking, help, trouble, stranded, bill, cheque, $, temporary, post.

You could also ask students if they think anything else is suspicious about the emails. They may notice that although there is no request for money in Example 2, they are asking for account details and providing a link which also does not use the bank's domain. Ask them what could happen if they followed the request to fill in account details.

If you have time...

Working with a partner, students make a list of four items. Three items on the list should have things in common and one should be the odd one out. Ensure students understand the rules of the game. Explain that there are no right or wrong answers. The game will help more-able students begin to identify patterns.

What success looks like: Students can correctly identify the odd one out.

▤ Test yourself...

FOUNDATION QUESTIONS

1 What is an algorithm? Answer: An algorithm is a set of instructions or rules we can use to carry out a task. Students should include the words 'instructions' or 'rules' in their answer.

2 Decompose the problem of getting dressed in the morning. Answer: A range of answers is possible, but students should identify that they will need to put on their underwear before outerwear, day clothes before coats, socks before shoes, etc.

EXTENSION QUESTIONS

3 What should you do if you receive a spam email? Answer: Learn to recognise spam in your email inboxes, and to delete or report it. Use an effective spam filter.

4 Give an example of how computational thinking relevant to everyday life. Answer: Students' own example including decomposition of a problem.

Learning outcomes

When they have completed this lesson students should be able to:

↗ use pattern recognition.

More-confident students will:

↗ be able to compare two problems.

Overview

In this lesson students will learn pattern recognition. Being able to identify and create patterns is an important tool in their computational thinking toolset. Students will:

- discover the importance of pattern recognition in solving real-world problems
- carry out a simple pattern recognition task as a class
- apply these new skills to the spam filter they are designing as the chapter project.

Language development

This lesson asks students to apply their knowledge of English to identify common word patterns in spam emails.

Before the lesson

You might want to share an enlarged version of the spam emails to help your classroom discussions.

The key words for this lesson are: pattern recognition. The words are highlighted in the text the first time they appear. Their definitions are included in the Key words box at the end of the lesson. You may want to review these words before the lesson.

 **Learn about...**

You will lead the first part of the lesson. Make sure students understand these ideas. You may ask them to make notes. You may use directed questioning to check understanding.

- What is a pattern? A pattern is finding the similarities and differences between things. Look at the example of the group of people in the Student Book. Ask students to suggest patterns in everyday life, such as patterns in nature (e.g. trees) or in equipment (e.g. balls for playing sports).
- We need to identify patterns when we solve real-world problems. Look at the example of Ignaz Semmelweiss in the Student Book.

- We can instruct computers to recognise patterns for us. Computational thinking uses pattern recognition to help solve problems.

⏻ **How to...**

In the second part of the lesson students complete an exercise under your guidance.

- Work with students to identify common words and features in the two mock spam emails from Lesson 1.1. The Student Book gives examples, such as 'bargain' and 'money'.
- Ask students why these words and features might seem suspicious. Students might suggest that unknown people are referring to money and that the language is too friendly.
- Discuss whether a bank is likely to send emails to their clients.

⊕ **Now you do it...**

In this lesson students are asked to refer back to their answers from the learning activity in Lesson 1.1. These answers form the basis of a decomposed problem. Students work in pairs to answer the questions in this activity.

What success looks like:

- Can you identify any patterns that might be useful? Answer: Both emails discuss money; neither email is addressed personally; individual words such as 'money' and individual signs such as '$' are used.
- What parts of the email could you think of as patterns? Answer: The sender's email address, greeting, body of the email can be seen as patterns.

🌐 **If you have time...**

Ask more-able students to write algorithms for making a cup of tea and a cup of coffee.

What success looks like:

- Which tasks are similar? Answer: Walk to the cupboard; take out a cup; place the cup on the table; pick up the kettle; take the kettle to the tap; fill the kettle with water; put the kettle on the table, switch on the kettle; pour boiled water into the cup.
- Which tasks are different? Answer: Take out the instant coffee; measure coffee into the cup; take out the teabag.
- Where could you use the same instructions in both processes? Answer: Walk to the cupboard; take out a cup; place the cup on the table; pick up the kettle; take the kettle to the tap; fill the kettle with water; put the kettle on the table, switch on the kettle; pour boiled water into the cup.

 Test yourself...

FOUNDATION QUESTIONS

1 What is pattern recognition? Answer: Pattern recognition is finding things that decomposed problems have in common.

2 Here is an image of some robots. Write any patterns you see. Answer: A range of answers is possible. Students should be expected to note similarities and differences. Similarities: All the robots have at least one eye; all the robots have a device for standing; all the robots can move; all the robots have something carrying out the function of a mouth. Differences: Not all of the robots have arms; each robot is a different colour; each robot is made of different shapes.

EXTENSION QUESTIONS

In Lesson 1.1, you decomposed the problem of designing and selling a new type of chocolate. Now imagine you are also going to design and sell a new type of cake.

3 Decompose the cake problem. Answer: A range of answers is possible. Many students may want to refer to the relevant text in Lesson 1.1 to provide a structure for their decomposition. The decomposition process can be repeated by replacing 'chocolate' with 'cake'.

4 Write the patterns you can see between the chocolate design process and the cake design process. Answer: Students should notice that the processes are almost identical.

1.3 Flow charts

pages 16–19

Learning outcomes

When they have completed this lesson students should be able to:

➚ describe an algorithm

➚ use a flow chart to describe your problem-solving.

More-confident students will:

➚ have considered how to apply the principles of flow charts beyond the lesson examples.

Overview

In this lesson students will be introduced to flow charts. Flow charts are an important way of representing computational thinking. We need to be able to represent our thinking to communicate it to others. Representing our thinking also helps make sure we have decomposed the problem properly. Students will learn about the basic components of flow charts. Students will also begin to describe their computational thinking on the spam filter problem by using a flow chart.

Language development

This lesson guide offers an additional lesson activity at the end, which will help the class develop a glossary to support language development as the chapter progresses.

Before the lesson

The key words for this lesson are: command, data flow chart, sequence and variable. The words are highlighted in the text the first time they appear. Their definitions are included in the Key words box at the end of the lesson. You may want to review these words before the lesson.

 ## Learn about...

You will lead the first part of the lesson. Make sure students understand these ideas. You may ask them to make notes. You may use directed questioning to check understanding.

- An algorithm is a set of instructions or rules we can use to carry out a task.
- Planning an algorithm carefully is likely to lead to an algorithm that is correct and efficient.

So far in this chapter students have written their algorithms as a long list of instructions. In the real world, people use flow charts and pseudocode to communicate their ideas. People use flow charts and pseudocode to test their algorithms before they implement these algorithms in computer code. (Students will learn more about pseudocode in *Matrix 2*.)

Many people find flow charts useful because they are a way of communicating ideas. Flow charts promote accuracy and make it easier to spot mistakes.

 ## How to...

In the second part of the lesson students complete an exercise under your guidance.

First, students are introduced to the most commonly-used flow chart symbols. You may want to spend time on the word 'variable', as this is an important concept in computing and science. The Khan Academy website has some helpful analogies on variables:

`www.khanacademy.org`

Work through the flow chart example with students.

 ## Now you do it...

Students make a flow chart to describe the program for their spam filter. Gaps in students' knowledge will become clear during this task. Before they complete the task, explain that they will be working on improving their flow chart for the remainder of this chapter. Students should not expect to produce a final or 'correct' version in this lesson. This lesson is an opportunity for students to learn that computing often requires trial and error ways of working.

Working in pairs, students can work through the

implications of the process-decision outlined in the Student Book. Ask students to think about what happens just before and just after these steps. Some students may prefer to begin with the 'start' command and progress forward.

What success looks like: Students begin to draft a flow chart for their spam filter.

Keep in your mind how the final flow charts might look to support your progress through the chapter. You can see this in Lesson 1.4 of this handbook.

End the lesson with a game that reinforces students' learning of new words. Put students into groups. Give each group a set of the key words cards you made earlier. Ask each group to create as many definitions for the words on the cards as they can in a five-minute period. Once the five minutes are over, ask each group to read out their definitions. Students could then create a classroom glossary to hang on the wall, which will support their language development.

 ## If you have time...

Students are asked to think of any disadvantages of using flow charts to show their computational thinking.

What success looks like:

- If a change has to be made, the flow chart would need to be drawn again.
- Complicated processes can be difficult to represent.
- Flow charts can be slow to create.
- Some people find flow charts forced—flow charts do not suit the way they approach computing problems.

 ## Test yourself...

FOUNDATION QUESTIONS

1 Why are flow charts useful in computational thinking? Answer: Flow charts are a way of communicating ideas to others; they make it easier to spot where there might be mistakes in a code; flow charts promote accuracy.

2 Draw and label the four main shapes we use to make flow charts. Answer: Students should draw the Start/Stop, Process, Decision and Input/Output shapes on page 17 of the Student Book.

EXTENSION QUESTIONS

3 Decompose the task of brushing your teeth. Answer: A range of answers is possible. Students should list many of these tasks: Pick up toothbrush; rinse toothbrush with water, pick up toothpaste, open toothpaste; squeeze toothpaste onto toothbrush; move toothbrush around mouth in circular motion; put down toothbrush; pick up glass of water; rinse mouth with water; spit out water; rinse toothbrush.

4   Make a flow chart to describe the process of brushing your teeth. Answer: Students' flowcharts

should include Start/Stop shapes and a series of processes. The most-able students could include a decision point when deciding whether to stop brushing teeth.

1.4 Selection and if... then... else statements

pages 20–23

Learning outcomes

When they have completed this lesson students should be able to:

↗   describe what selection is

↗   use if... then... else to navigate through a problem.

More-confident students will:

↗   have applied their understanding of selection to real-life computer program examples.

Overview

In this lesson students will be introduced to two important tools in designing algorithms: sequencing and selection. Students will learn when it is useful to use these tools and how to represent them in a flow chart. The lesson encourages students to think about the decision points in their spam filter flow charts. Students will also think about choosing sequencing or selection tools.

Language development

Students are introduced to three key words in this lesson. They are all words that are used more widely in English, but have technical meanings in computing. Sequencing is the order in which steps or tasks are carried out. Selection happens when a step in the algorithm is reached where the program has two or more possibilities of what to do next. Implement means to put an algorithm into action. You may want to spend time comparing the ways in which these words are used in English and the ways in which they are used in computing.

Before the lesson

The key words for this lesson are: implement, selection and sequencing. The words are highlighted the first time they appear in the text. Their definitions are included in the Key words box at the end of the lesson. You may want to review these words before the lesson.

The next section of this handbook describes a dominoes game that you may want to play in the first part of the lesson, '**Learn about...** '. If you want to play the dominoes game, you will need dominoes, or rectangular prism wooden blocks of identical size. If not, you may want to share a suitable YouTube video of a domino run.

Learn about...

You will lead the first part of the lesson. Start with a game. Put students into groups. Give each group up to twenty dominoes or blocks. Ask each group to set up a 'domino run' by placing each block on its smallest end, in a line, with about one centimetre between the blocks. Ask students to set off the domino run by pushing the block on one end into the block next to it.

Explain that the domino run is like a sequence. Each block carries out its own task in a particular order.

Now ask students to create a run with a single line that then branches out into two lines.

Explain that this is like selection. The algorithm has a decision point with two (or more) possibilities of what to do next.

Make sure students understand these ideas. You may ask them to make notes. You may use directed questioning to check understanding.

- **Sequence:** A sequence is the order in which steps or tasks are carried out.
- **Selection:** Selection happens when two or more things could occur in a step in a program. We can talk about selection as a decision, for example a computer avatar could decide to walk down a path. We can talk about selection as a question, for example by asking whether a robot has done an activity enough times.

How to...

In the second part of the lesson students complete an exercise under your guidance.

This section in the Student Book explains how to implement selection in an algorithm. Building on the example from Lesson 1.3, it introduces students to three important ideas.

- We can use 'yes' and 'no' to help our algorithm decide which path to take. If the answer to the decision point is yes, the algorithm can be instructed to take a particular path. If the answer to the decision point is no, the algorithm can be instructed to take a different path.

- We can use `if... then` to say this in a more elegant way. If the answer to our decision is yes, then the algorithm can be instructed to take a particular path. If the answer to the decision is no, then the algorithm can be instructed to take a different path.
- If there are more than two choices we may want to use `if... then... else`.

Students will build on these ideas during the programming chapters (Chapter 2, App Inventor and Chapter 4, Introducing Python) in the Student Book.

In this lesson students apply what they know about selection to their developing flow charts. Here is an example of what a simple spam filter flow chart might look like by the end of the chapter. Students are not expected to reach this stage in this lesson.

Now you do it...

In this activity, students work with a partner to apply what they know about selection to their flow chart showing the design of a spam filter.

What success looks like: When they reach their decision points, they should think of the possible

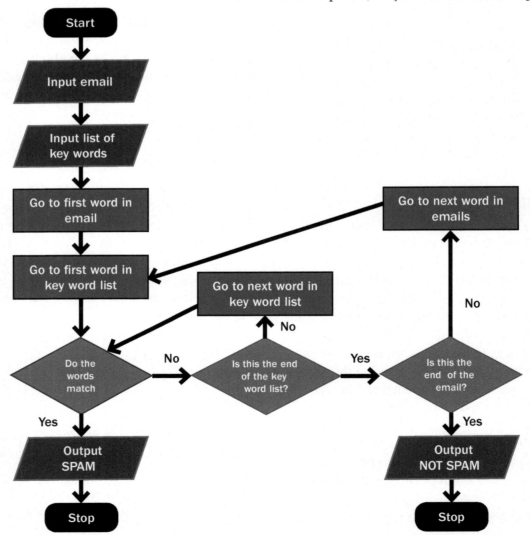

answers to the question. They should show the different paths their design could take. Students' answers might include: a computer game where an avatar has a choice of more than one route to take; a logistics program choosing routes for delivery vehicles or ambulances; an online survey.

 If you have time...

Students are asked to think about other computer programs where selection might be useful.

What success looks like: A range of answers is possible, including: a computer game where an avatar has a choice of more than one route to take; a logistics program choosing routes for delivery vehicles or ambulances; an online survey.

 Test yourself...

FOUNDATION QUESTIONS

1 Finish this sentence: Selection happens when... Answer: ...a step in the algorithm is reached where

the program has two or more possibilities of what to do next.

2 What does implement mean? Answer: Implement means to put algorithms into action.

EXTENSION QUESTIONS

3 Work with a partner. Imagine you are programming a game. Your avatar is walking along a woodland path. The avatar sees three paths ahead. Decompose the problem. Are there obstacles on any of the paths? Is there treasure on any of the paths? Answer: A range of answers is possible. Expect students to describe at least one obstacle or reward for the three paths.

4 Create a simple flow chart that shows what your avatar sees when looking down each one of the paths. Answer: A range of answers is possible, depending on the obstacles or rewards students have described in Question 3. Expect students to use selection constructs. Most students will use `if... then`. More able students will use `if... then... else`.

1.5 Loops

pages 24–27

Learning outcomes

When they have completed this lesson students should be able to:

↗ describe iteration

↗ use loops in a program.

More-confident students will:

↗ extend their understanding of loops beyond the lesson.

Overview

In this lesson students will learn about the construct of iteration, and how to use loops in computing to show iteration. Students will apply their understanding to their spam filter designs. By the end of the lesson, students should be close to completing their flow charts. Students will evaluate these flow charts in the final lesson of the chapter.

Language development

This lesson introduces students to the idea of iteration and the concept 'to loop'. These words are used widely in English, but have technical meanings in computing. Iteration means repeating a step or task in an algorithm or computer program. To loop means to go back to a previous step. Looping happens in iterations.

Before the lesson

You will need to prepare pieces of string before the lesson to carry out the language reinforcement activity.

Before the lesson evaluate each student's progress against the chapter objectives. During the lesson work with any students who have not yet created a flow chart for a spam filter. Working with these students will ensure they have something that can be evaluated during the final lesson.

The key words for this lesson are: iteration and loop. The words are highlighted the first time they appear in the text. Their definitions are included in the Key words box at the end of the lesson. You may want to review these words before the lesson.

 ## Learn about...

You will lead the first part of the lesson. Make sure students understand these ideas. You may ask them to make notes. You may use directed questioning to check understanding.

- **Constructs:** Constructs are the tools we use to build algorithms. Students already know about two constructs: sequencing and selection.

- **Iteration:** Iteration is another construct. Iteration makes it possible for us to tell an algorithm to repeat a step more than once. We show iteration in a flow chart using loops. We can show a loop in a flow chart using an arrow.

If students need more reinforcement of the language, give each student a piece of string. Ask them to place all the pieces of string end to end. The pieces of string are now in a sequence. Now ask each student to make a loop by joining the ends of their own piece of string. Place the loops next to each other. Explain to students that the loops are iterating (repeating).

 ## How to...

In the second part of the lesson students complete an exercise under your guidance. The exercise is based on a computer game, in which an avatar looks down three paths in a wood. Each path contains treasure. The avatar is instructed to walk down each path, collect the treasure, and return to the start.

Move through the flow chart example step by step (page 25).

- Start.
- There are three paths ahead of the avatar.

- Set the first path as the current path. Ask students why they think this might be useful. They should note how it enables the avatar to repeat an action with the next path.
- Instruct the avatar to walk down the current path, collect the treasure, and return to the intersection.
- At the decision point, ask whether the current path is the last path. If the current path is *not* the last path, then the next path becomes the current path, and the avatar loops back. If the current path *is* the last path, then stop.

Discuss the way the loop makes it possible to run the program for three paths or more. There is no need to write out the actions many times over.

 ## Now you do it...

Students work in pairs to adapt their flow chart to include a loop. Students should see how the loop makes repeated actions, such as searching for key words. The completed flow chart in this handbook (Lesson 1.4) shows how students could respond to the questions in the Student Book.

What success looks like: Students' answers might include these points.

- There are repeated actions searching for multiple key words in each email. There are also repeated actions in searching more than one email.
- Loops are an efficient way to carry out repeated actions without having to write the same instruction many times.

Encourage students to redraw their flow chart so it can be clearly read by others for the next lesson. Work with less able students to complete a flow chart together.

 ## If you have time...

This extension activity refers to the 'How to' section for this lesson and the test question in Lesson 1.4. The extension activity asks students to think about what changes they might make to the flow chart if there were more than one path.

What success looks like: More able students should realise that they would not need to change their flow chart for ten paths, or for a million. This is why abstraction, iteration and looping are useful in computing, and why they are essential computational thinking skills.

Test yourself...

FOUNDATION QUESTIONS

1 Complete the words naming the three algorithm constructs we use in computational thinking. Answer: Sequencing; Selection; Iteration.

2 Why is iteration important in programming? Answer: Iteration makes it possible to repeat a command or action many times without needing to write or code it many times.

EXTENSION QUESTIONS

3 Think of an example of a computer program that would need to use loops. Answer: Students could suggest a range of programs, including software that measures and tracks the weather, stock markets and computer gaming.

4 Using your own words, describe what is happening in this flow chart. Answer: Students are told that the flow chart describes the actions of the factory robot. Their responses should contain these points.

○ Robot aligns with Point A.

○ At the decision point, ask if there is a box for the robot to pick up. If the answer is NO, then stop. Some less able students might say 'if there is no box, then stop'. If the answer is YES, then pick up the box. Some less able students might say 'if there is a box, pick it up'.

○ Move the box to Point B.

○ Put down the box.

○ Move back to Point A. Loop back to the alignment step.

 ## Evaluation

pages 28–31

Learning outcomes

When they have completed this lesson students should be able to:

↗ evaluate other people's work

↗ give helpful feedback.

More-confident students will:

↗ have applied their feedback to their work.

Overview

This final lesson gives students the opportunity to complete their work, evaluate others' work and learn to provide effective feedback. You may want to use this lesson to complete formative assessments and give small group or one-to-one support.

Language development

Students will learn to use everyday English words to describe the evaluation process. However, the word 'elegant' may be confusing for students with English as an additional language. Elegant has a different meaning in computing to the one it has in everyday English. Elegant means that an algorithm is clear for someone else to understand. You can discuss the meaning of this word during the lesson.

Before the lesson

Be aware which students will need to use this lesson to complete their spam filter design, and which students are likely to complete the extension task.

The key words for this lesson are: criteria, efficient, elegant and fit for purpose. The words are highlighted the first time they appear in the text. Their definitions are included in the Key words box at the end of the lesson. You may want to review these words before the lesson, particularly the word, 'elegant' as this has a different meaning in computing.

If you think students will find the words used during this lesson difficult, make sets of cards from the set of key word cards for this lesson (see the Preparation section) and create a matching set of definition cards. Have several copies of each set of words for each pack of cards you make. Each pack will be used by two students, playing in pairs, for the snap game suggested in the first part of the lesson.

 ## Learn about...

You will lead the first part of the lesson. Make sure students understand these ideas. You may ask them to make notes. You may use directed questioning to check understanding.

- Once we have designed an algorithm, we can evaluate it to see if it is fit for purpose.
- An algorithm can be hard to evaluate when we have been working closely on it. To solve this problem we can ask other people to evaluate our work, using agreed criteria.
- An algorithm that is fit for purpose is elegant, efficient, decomposed and correct.
- Elegant means that an algorithm is clear for someone else to understand. Efficient means that an algorithm is doing the best work for the least effort. Fit for purpose means that an algorithm or program does the job it is supposed to do. We use criteria to judge whether a program is doing the job we need it to do.

If students find these words hard, play a snap game. Place students in pairs. Students take turns to put cards on the table. When the word matches the definition, the student identifying the match calls out 'snap'. The student can then pick up all the cards on the table. The student with the most cards wins the game. This game will help students who are finding the language difficult to practise their understanding in a fun way.

 ## How to...

In the second part of the lesson students complete an exercise under your guidance. The example is a simple algorithm for making a cup of tea.

Discuss the first algorithm with students. Use the key words for the lesson to describe why the algorithm is not fit for purpose.

- Look at the properly decomposed algorithm beneath the tea pot diagram. Compare and contrast the differences between the algorithms with students. Point out that although the second algorithm is longer, it addresses the criteria more completely than the short algorithm. The short algorithm was not fit for purpose.
- Explain how to give effective feedback. Encourage students to use sentence openings such as these.
  - 'You could improve this by... '
  - 'I like the way you have... '
  - 'If you added....this algorithm would be more elegant/fit-for-purpose/efficient/correct.'
- You may want to give some silly examples to show students which behaviours and language to avoid. Here are some examples.
  - 'This is good.' (unclear)
  - 'I think you have done this wrong.' (personal and subjective)
  - Any statement followed by 'but'.

 ## Now you do it...

Work as a class to develop three evaluation criteria for the spam filter algorithms that students have completed.

Still working in pairs, students who have completed their algorithms can evaluate each others' work, giving effective feedback. Ask students to write down their feedback so you can assess it after the lesson. While students write their feedback, you can offer small group or one-to-one support to those who have not finished their algorithms.

What success looks like: Students complete their algorithms and evaluate each others' work, giving effective feedback.

If you have time...

The Student Book asks more-able students to implement the feedback they have been given. If students do not agree with the feedback, encourage them to say why they do not agree.

What success looks like: Students implement their feedback and can discuss it, giving reasons for their answers.

 Test yourself...

FOUNDATION QUESTIONS

1 What criteria can we use to judge whether an algorithm is fit for purpose? Answer: decomposed, correct, efficient, elegant.

2 What are the characteristics of good feedback? Answer: Keep it about the work; show where things are working well; be specific.

EXTENSION QUESTIONS

3 Summarise the main strengths and weaknesses of the spam filter you have designed. Answer: Answers will depend on the characteristics of the individual algorithms students have designed. Students' responses to this question should take into account the four characteristics of a fit-for-purpose algorithm outlined in this lesson: decomposition, correctness, elegance, efficiency.

4 How could you address the weaknesses? Answer: Answers will depend upon the characteristics of the individual algorithms students have designed. Students' responses should demonstrate self-awareness and the ability to be critical about their own work.

Review what students have learned about computational thinking

pages 32–33

The test questions and assessment activities in the Student Book give you an opportunity to evaluate students' understanding. The questions are shown here with possible answers.

 Model answers to test questions

1 What is computational thinking? Answer: Computational thinking is making sure we understand problems and thinking up possible solutions.

2 Why is computational thinking important to programming? Answer: Computational thinking is important because it helps us: understand problems, find the right solutions to problems, communicate problems and solutions to others, solve problems together.

3 Give an example of how we can use computational thinking in everyday life. Answer: We might use computational thinking to: plan a trip, plan a written piece of work, make a meal, create a piece of artwork, set up a business.

4 What are the three constructs you can use to design algorithms? Answer: a) iteration, b) selection, c) sequencing.

5 Explain what the following words and phrases mean using your own words. Answer: a) pattern recognition: finding the similarities and differences between things; b) sequencing: the order in which steps or tasks are carried out; c) selection: happens when you reach a step in the algorithm where the program has two or more possibilities of what to do next; d) iteration: repeating a step or task in an algorithm or computer program.

6 What is a loop? Answer: Most students' answers to this question should include an explanation that looping means returning to a previous step. More able students may place this in the context of iteration.

7 Give an example of an algorithm where a loop would be useful. Answer: A loop would be useful: when searching for a key word in a long text or when a robot needs to repeat the same action. For example, an underwater robotic vehicle might need to move back and forth across the ocean floor when looking for something.

8 a) Think back to the algorithm evaluation jigsaw. Which four words can you use to help decide whether an algorithm is fit for purpose? On a separate sheet of paper, draw the jigsaw and write one of the four words you have chosen on each piece. Answer: Decomposed, efficient, correct, elegant.

9 Design a poster to tell other students about the dangers of spam. Include this information on your poster.

   a) What is spam? Answer: Email spam involves sending messages to many people who have not asked for the emails to be sent.

   b) What is a spam filter? Answer: A spam filter is a computer program that spots unsolicited email. It can stop unsolicited email from getting into your inbox.

   c) How does a spam filter work? Answer: A spam filter searches for key words and phrases in every email sent to your inbox. A spam filter identifies emails that are likely to be untrustworthy.

   d) What should you do if you receive a spam email? Answer: Most students should give at least one of these answers. More able students may give both answers.

   ○ Delete or report spam email.

   ○ Use an effective spam filter.

10 Look at the poster another student has made. Evaluate the poster by telling the other student one thing that has been done well, and one thing that the student could do to improve the poster. Answer: Student feedback on the poster could be written or spoken, depending on your knowledge of the class. The feedback should:

   ○ be specific

   ○ be focused on the work and not include any personal negative comments

   ○ show where things have been done well.

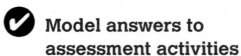 Model answers to assessment activities

Starter activity

Students are given a choice of three meals to make: a salad, a boiled egg or a sandwich. Students are asked to choose one meal and decompose the task.

What success looks like:

Making a sandwich is the easiest of the three tasks. The task does not specify a sandwich filling or type of bread. Answer: Expect to see some or all of these decomposed tasks: Place bread on breadboard; Fetch knife; Cut two slices of bread; Fetch butter (or other choice of filling); Spread butter on bread; Place one piece of bread on the other.

Making a salad is a more challenging task, as students will need to include a loop in their flowchart later in the assessment. Answer: Expect to see some or all of these decomposed tasks: Choose type of salad; Fetch ingredients from the fridge, place on table; Fetch chopping board and knife, place on table; Fetch a bowl, place on table; Chop vegetables; Place vegetables in bowl.

Expect more-able students to break the task down further if necessary. For example, they might include more detail on ingredients, or include ingredients that require cooking, e.g. rice.

Boiling an egg is a more challenging task. More able students may choose to include decision points and loops at up to two points in their flow charts later in the assessment. Answer: Expect to see some or all of these decomposed tasks: Take pot out of cupboard; Pour water into pot; Place top on stove; Boil water; Fetch egg; Place egg in pot of water; Record time; Check time; If correct time has elapsed, remove egg. If not, go back to check time; Place egg in egg cup or remove egg shell.

Intermediate activity

Students are asked to draw a flow chart to show how you would make their chosen meal.

What success looks like: All students should include most or all of these elements in their flow charts.

Extension activity

Students are asked to evaluate the flow chart made by a partner.

What success looks like: The written feedback they provide should include the characteristics of helpful feedback. They should:

● be specific
● be focused on the work, and not include any personal negative comments
● show where things have been done well.

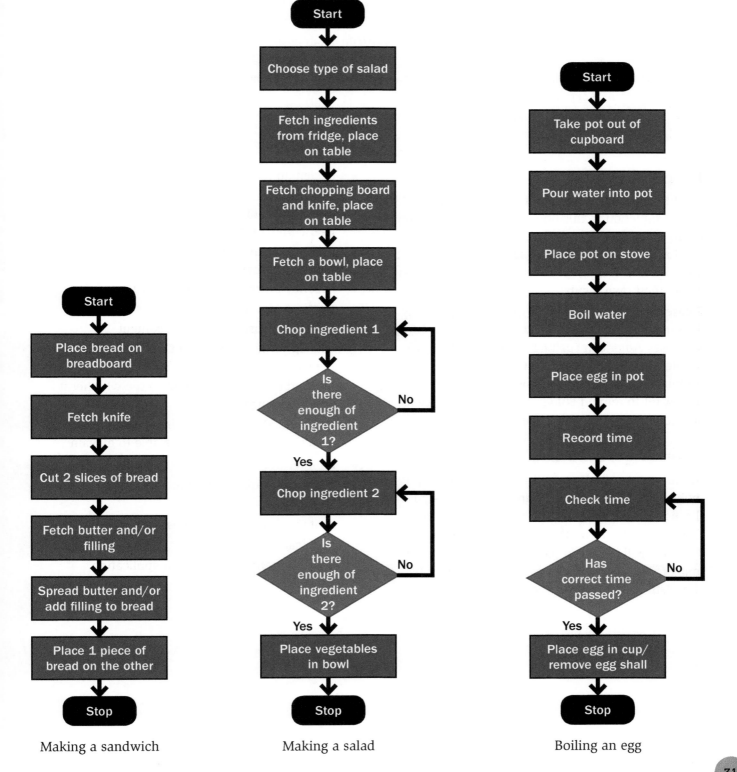

Making a sandwich   Making a salad   Boiling an egg

Curriculum coverage

This chapter covers part or all of the requirements for the Computing program of study (age 11–14) for England:

↗ use programming languages to solve a variety of computational problems

↗ create digital artefacts for a given audience.

This chapter also covers these main requirements for the Computing at School (CAS) Progression Pathways (for a full list of requirements met, see pages 9–10 of this handbook):

↗ understand that programming bridges the gap between algorithmic solutions and computers

↗ use a range of operators and expressions (e.g. Boolean), and apply them in the context of program control

↗ detect and correct syntactical errors.

Preparation

Read the section, 'Preparing to use App Inventor' in the introduction to this book (page 12) before you begin this topic. Be sure you know how students can log on to App Inventor. Make sure you have IDs and logins to assign, or be ready to help students create their own logins.

Please be aware of American spelling when using App Inventor. App Inventor was made in the USA, so it uses American spellings. For example, it uses 'Center' instead of 'Centre', 'Color' instead of 'Colour' and 'Initialize' instead of 'Initialise'. You may want to remind students of this difference as you come across words spelled in US style.

Learning outcomes

In this chapter students will make a simple app for a mobile phone. They will be guided step by step through every part of this activity. The app will display an ID card on the screen of a mobile phone. The card will include a name and a photo (or other image). The card will be password protected. By completing this chapter students will be able to:

- design an interface with buttons, labels and text boxes
- make an event-driven program that reacts to user commands
- display text and images as output from a computer program
- describe syntax errors and error messages
- duplicate and delete code blocks
- upload and use multimedia content
- use logical tests and the `if` command to control the computer
- test and evaluate a program to see whether it meets user needs.

Students will also develop their understanding of computer systems. They will be able to explain:

- an interface
- event-driven programming
- a trigger
- syntax errors and error messages
- a logical test
- the importance of testing an application.

Make a mobile app

Talk about...

The discussion is an activity you can do offline. You could use this activity any time to vary the pace of lessons and encourage students to reflect on their learning.

1 Apps: There are millions of apps available to use on mobile phones. What apps do you know? What are the most useful apps? Are there any apps you would like that haven't been invented yet?

   ○ If students have smartphones and/or tablets you can look at examples of apps that they use. If most students do not own these devices, you could provide examples of screens of phones and tablets. For example, you might do a presentation, create a hand-out, or simply show a phone to the class.

   ○ Encourage students to talk about the apps they know, like, and use. If students don't use phones, encourage them to talk about what they know or imagine can be done with phones.

   ○ Finally, looking to the future, what phone apps might students like to have one day? An app that would control a robot? An app that would do their homework? An app that would help them know what to say in social situations? Young people are imaginative and will probably think of many interesting ideas.

2 Proof of ID: You often have to prove your ID, for example, when you go into the school building. What ways are there for a person to prove his or her ID? What are the advantages and disadvantages of the different methods?

   ○ The Proof of ID activity encourages students to think about the social and personal implications of advances in technology.

How can we prove our identity? We can do it with or without technology. For example, by showing a pass to a person. What new technologies might come into existence? The different methods of proving ID have advantages and disadvantages. These different methods are summarised in the table.

Offline activity

The offline 'Design an ID card' activity gives students a chance to do creative work without using computers. You could use this activity to introduce the App Inventor lessons.

This task will give students a chance to reflect on interface design without having to worry about using design software that they may be unfamiliar with. Their creative ideas will not be limited by their technical skills.

In this chapter students will make an on-screen ID card on the computer. The design of the app will be slightly limited because students are still learning to use the interface design software. In this offline activity students can work in groups or individually to create more diverse and interesting screen designs using pen and paper.

Make this a future-looking activity, and tell students they can add any technical features they like—even ones that aren't generally available at the moment. This is an imaginative and creative exercise.

Word cloud

The Word cloud contains all the key words that have been highlighted and defined in Key word boxes throughout the lesson. The key words for this chapter are: app, input, output, logical test, syntax error, multimedia, event-driven programming, upload, syntax, property, text property, trigger, evaluate, visual programming, right-click, client.

	Password	Biometric	ID card
What is it?	A text or number sequence you enter into the computer.	The computer measures some feature of your body such as your fingerprint or eye scan.	A card which may have your name and photo on it. Sometimes it has a magnetic strip or computer chip in it.
Advantages	Easy and cheap to use.	People can't steal your biometric features.	Can be read by a person or a computerised system.
Disadvantages	People sometimes forget their password. Some passwords are easy to guess.	Needs expensive equipment.	Can be lost. If it is stolen another person can use it to pretend to be you.

Learning outcomes

When they have completed this lesson students should be able to:

↗ design an interface with buttons and labels.

More-confident students will:

↗ vary object properties and evaluate the effect of these changes.

Overview

This is the first lesson using App Inventor. Students do not need to have any prior learning in programming, either using App Inventor or in any other language. In this lesson they will design an interface. Students will do no programming in this lesson. However, the lesson will introduce them to using the software.

Language development

Important words introduced in this lesson include app (short for 'application software') and the concepts of input and output. The interface of an app is what the user sees when he or she uses the app. The interface handles input (the user clicking on buttons or typing text) and output (the messages and displays from the software).

'Property' has a technical sense in this context. A property of an object is any characteristic or feature of an object, such as its size or colour. In this lesson students will change the properties of objects on the interface.

Before the lesson

In or before the lesson, each student needs an 'App Inventor' login identity. These identities are linked to Gmail accounts. You could organise a Gmail name and App Inventor login for every student. Or, you could have a standard set of 20 or 30 logins which you use with different classes. In either case you must ensure students are ready to log in and use App Inventor.

This stage may need a large part of the lesson to complete. The time taken will depend on the ability and confidence of students, and how much you can prepare in advance.

The key words for this lesson are: app, input, output, property and text property. The words are highlighted in the text the first time they appear.

Their definitions are included in the Key words box at the end of the lesson. You may want to review these words before the lesson.

⌘ Learn about...

You will lead the first part of the lesson. Make sure students understand these ideas. You may ask them to make notes. You may use directed questioning to check understanding.

- **Interface:** The interface is the feature that allows us to interact with the computer. In a mobile app it is usually a touch screen. Explain the difference between input and output.
- **Interface design:** Ask students to consider what features of a touch screen interface are used for input and output. Examples are buttons, labels, sounds, menus, vibration and speech.

⏻ How to...

In the second part of the lesson students complete an exercise under your guidance.

1   **Start App Inventor:** Guide students through the process of logging on to the App Inventor website and/or creating a new user ID. If you are going to use the emulator to run the finished app, then it is best to load it before you begin.

2   **Start a project:** Help students to start a new project. Each student must give the work file a suitable name, for example, IDCard. If students are sharing a user login with other students, make sure they include their initials in the file name.

3   **Designer screen:** Talk through the four features of the Designer screen. Guide students as they use these four features to create a simple interface. Students will use each feature in turn from left to right.

   ○ Palette—drag objects (a button and a label) onto the viewer
   ○ Viewer—the objects appear here forming a simple interface

○ Components—rename the objects as `IDButton` and `NameLabel`
○ Set object properties—change the text property of the objects as shown in the Student Book

When students rename the button and the label you can explain why we choose these names. The names show the function of the object (e.g. to show your ID) and the type of object (e.g. a button).

4 **Run the app:** Practise using the emulator and/or the method for running the app on a mobile device before the lesson. Help students to use one of these methods to run the completed app. You may need to deal with problems, but the activity is fairly straightforward. When the connection is made successfully students will see the interface they made on the screen of a mobile device (or emulator).

⊕ Now you do it...

If students have followed your instructions, they should have created an interface with suitable properties and ran the app. If necessary, give struggling students more than one lesson to complete this activity. Give more-confident students the extension activity as you support those who need help.

What success looks like: Successful students will have produced work that looks like the interface shown in the Student Book (page 38).

🌐 If you have time...

The extension activity gives students the opportunity to explore independently. There are several object properties such as font, object size and colour. By changing these object properties, students can vary the appearance of the interface. This is an open-ended activity that will give more-confident students a feeling of control over their work. The timing of the activity is flexible and will allow you to direct your main attention to struggling students.

What success looks like: The experience of changing object properties is the important thing. Students can choose whatever colours and designs they want.

📄 Test yourself...

FOUNDATION QUESTIONS

1 What is the difference between input and output? Answer: Input: Signals and information that go into the computer, for example, from the user touching the screen. Output: Signals and information that come out of the computer, for example, a screen display.

2 Every object in App Inventor has properties. List three properties that an object might have. Answer: There is a range of possible answers, but students might say: text, size, and colour of the object. For more answers look at the Properties section of the App Inventor Designer screen.

EXTENSION QUESTIONS

3 The interface you made has two objects. Which object is used for input and which for output? Answer: The two objects are a button and a label. The button is used for input. The label is used for output.

4 You changed the names of two objects. What makes a good name for an object? Answer: A good object name will tell you what type of object it is (e.g. a button). A good object name will also tell you what the object's job is (what the object is used for).

Learning outcomes

When they have completed this lesson students should be able to:

↗ make an event-driven program that reacts to user commands

↗ display text as output from a computer program.

More-confident students will:

↗ extend and adapt the program code to make it carry out additional actions.

Overview

Students have created an interface. However, there is no code attached to it. The interface doesn't 'do' anything. In this lesson students will create a simple block of code. App Inventor is a visual programming language, so students will make the code by fitting coloured blocks together. The code will change the interface into an active app. When students click on the ID Button on the interface, their name will appear on the screen. Students can use any name they like. Some students may choose funny names. Others may choose the names of famous people. As long as their choices are not offensive, this will not change the learning value of the activity.

Language development

Key words introduced in this lesson include the concept of software being event-driven. This is technical vocabulary. Most students will not know this term, regardless of their language background.

App Inventor is a visual programming language, so students can use visual cues to build program code. However, the text on the blocks is in English. Students may need support if they are still developing English skills.

Before the lesson

Practise the work in advance so you are confident. Make sure you have the details of the login ID and password for every student.

In this chapter each piece of work builds on the previous lesson. Make sure students save their work between lessons.

- If you have saved your app from the previous lesson, open it. Be ready to continue working on the app as you show how to add functionality.

- Students should also have their saved work ready for further development. If any students have not completed the previous work they must complete it before continuing with this lesson. By working from the Student Book, students who are behind can catch up with the rest of the class.

This advice applies to all lessons in this section.

The key words for this lesson are: event-driven, visual programming and trigger. The words are highlighted in the text the first time they appear. Their definitions are included in the Key words box at the end of the lesson. You may want to review these words before the lesson.

⌘ Learn about...

You will lead the first part of the lesson. Make sure students understand the concept of event-driven programming and the idea of a trigger. You may ask them to make notes. You may use directed questioning to check understanding.

- **Event-driven programming:** Modern touch-screen apps often have a visual interface with buttons, icons and other features. The app responds when the user touches the screen. Touching the screen is an event. Until the event happens the code does not do anything. Code which only works in response to an event is called 'event-driven' programming.

- **Trigger:** An event that makes the computer do something is called a trigger. All code in event-driven programming is linked to a trigger. In this activity the trigger for the code is when the user clicks on IDButton.

⏻ How to...

In the second part of the lesson students complete an exercise under your guidance.

- **Open the Blocks screen:** Show students how to open the second App Inventor screen, which is the Blocks screen. Explain the difference between the Blocks screen and the Designer screen. Students will need to use both screens to create a working app.

- **Choose ID button:** Take particular care with this activity as it is the first time students will select a program code block. The menu at the left of the screen shows the different components of the interface. Find IDButton. When students click on this, a series of blocks linked to this button will appear. Find the block `when IDButton. Click` and drag it onto the Viewer area.
- **Set NameLabel text:** Students must drag another block onto the Viewer area and fit it inside the space in the previous block. App Inventor works by joining blocks together. Take time to make sure all students get this right.
- **Add new text:** Finally students select a blank Text block and fit it into the developing code. Students can type a name or other text into this block. This text will be displayed on the interface when the user clicks IDButton.
- **Run the program:** Students know how to run the App Inventor program on an emulator or mobile device from Lesson 2.1. Students should do this now. By clicking on the button, students will trigger the code they just made. Their name will appear on the screen.

Now you do it...

If students have followed your instructions, they should have created a working app which responds to user actions. Students who are more comfortable working slowly may take more than one lesson to achieve this. Give more-confident students the extension activity as you support those who need help.

What success looks like: The Student Book shows the assembled code on page 42. Successful work will match this. The code will work so that students will be able to run the app.

If you have time...

The extension activity gives students the opportunity to explore independently. Students can add extra labels to the interface and add code to the program so that text is shown in these extra labels. For example, the labels could display age, email address, phone number.

What success looks like: A student who has added one or more labels to the interface, which change when they press the button, has completed the extension activity.

Test yourself...

FOUNDATION QUESTIONS

1 Why do you think App Inventor is sometimes called a visual programming language? Answer: App Inventor is called a visual programming language because you make the code by combining visual elements: blocks which fit together.

2 The code you made is triggered when an event happens. What event triggers the action? Answer: The user clicks on (or touches) IDButton.

EXTENSION QUESTIONS

3 Explain the purpose of the Designer screen and the Blocks screen in App Inventor. What is the difference between them? Answer: The exact phrases students use may vary. The points they should make are: the Designer screen lets you create an interface by adding components and setting their properties; the Blocks screen lets you create program code by fitting code blocks together.

4 When the trigger happens, what action is carried out by the computer? Answer: Students should correctly describe the result of the working app. For example, 'The screen shows the text that you entered in the program code' or 'Your name appears on the app screen'.

Learning outcomes

When they have completed this lesson students should be able to:

↗ describe syntax and error messages

↗ duplicate and delete code blocks.

More-confident students will:

↗ change the properties of the interface to add their own personal touches.

Overview

Students who have completed Lessons 2.1 and 2.2 have created an interface and simple program code. In this lesson students will extend the interface. They will add a 'reset' button, which will blank out the name on the screen. This provides an opportunity to practise skills learned in previous lessons, as well as extending understanding.

Language development

Important words introduced in this lesson include syntax, which has a technical meaning for programmers. In English language usage, syntax means the rules of language, such as grammar. In programming, syntax means the rules of a computer language such as App Inventor or Python.

Before the lesson

The key words for this lesson are: right-click, syntax and syntax error. The words are highlighted in the text the first time they appear. Their definitions are included in the Key words box at the end of the lesson. You may want to review these words before the lesson.

⌘ Learn about...

You will lead the first part of the lesson. Make sure students understand these ideas. You may ask them to make notes. You may use directed questioning to check understanding.

- **Syntax errors:** Syntax errors are mistakes that break the rules of the programming language. Syntax errors will stop your program from working. Emphasise to students that making errors is part of the task of a programmer. If you spot and correct errors, you are working effectively.

- **Error messages:** Explain that error messages tell you when you have made a syntax error. A good error message will often also explain the error.

As you demonstrate the programming activity you will cause an error message to appear temporarily. Use the error message as a learning aid.

 How to...

In the second part of the lesson students complete a learning exercise under your guidance.

- **Add a Reset button:** Add a button, rename it and change the text property. This action gives students a chance to practise skills they learned in Lesson 2.2. Move to the Blocks screen and drag the `when ResetButton.Click` block onto the Viewer.

- **Duplicate blocks:** Programmers often make a copy of a block of code that works, and then adapt the copy to carry out a new task. Duplicating blocks saves time and reduces errors. Show students how to duplicate the `NameLabel.Text` block by right-clicking on the block and choosing Duplicate from the drop-down menu.

  ○ Note: Make sure students choose the correct block for duplication. Students need to duplicate the green block called `set NameLabel.Text`. The pink Text block will automatically be duplicated too.

  ○ Note: Once the block has been duplicated, students must fit the duplicate copy inside the `when ResetButton.Click` box. Students must then delete the words in the pink Text block so it just has a blank space.

- **Delete blocks:** To demonstrate deletion of unwanted blocks, make an extra block and drag it to the delete bin. If students make a mistake in duplication, simply delete any incorrect blocks and start again.

○ Note: App Inventor does not let you fit blocks together the wrong way round—they won't fit. This helps avoid syntax errors. Click the message 'Show Warnings' at the bottom right of the Viewer screen to see detailed error messages linked to the blocks.

Now you do it...

Students add a Reset button as described. Students make code to go with the Reset button using duplication. Students should pay attention to syntax errors and look out for error messages.

What success looks like: The Student Book shows the correct outcome of this activity (on page 45).

If you have time...

The extension activity gives students the opportunity to explore independently. The Student Book recommends simple amendments, but no guidance is given. The correct approach to the two tasks is the following.

- To change the properties of the Reset button, open the Designer screen, select the Reset button and look in the Properties window. Make any changes and check the effect on the appearance of the interface. Any feature of the button, for example colour or size, may be changed by the student.

- To change the text that is displayed when the Reset button is clicked, go back to the Blocks screen. Find the ResetButton block. Change the contents of the pink Text block from a blank to the words STAND BY.

What success looks like: The properties of the reset button should be changed in some way and the when the reset button is clicked the text should say STANDBY.

Test yourself...

FOUNDATION QUESTIONS

1 What is program syntax? Answer: Syntax means the rules of a language. Program syntax means the rules of a computer programming language.

2 'A good programmer never makes errors'. Discuss this statement—is it true? Answer: The statement is not true. Even good programmers do make mistakes. The key factor that makes a good programmer is spotting and fixing errors.

EXTENSION QUESTIONS

3 Explain how error messages and warning messages may help a programmer do their job. Answer: Warnings and error message help programmers spot and fix errors. A good error message will say what problem has been discovered and where it is in the program. A good message might also tell you how to fix it.

4 Explain how duplicating or copying a block of code may help a programmer do their job. Answer: Duplicating code means that programmers can re-use a block of code they have already used for a similar purpose. The code is slightly changed for the new purpose. Duplicating code saves time and reduces the chance of errors because the programmers are using work they have got right before.

Learning outcomes

When they have completed this lesson students should be able to:

↗ upload and use multimedia content.

More-confident students will:

↗ add additional code, working independently from simple instructions.

Overview

Students have made an interface that displays their name. Now they will extend the interface to display a photo or other suitable image. Adding a photo to the interface will give students experience of working with multimedia content.

Language development

Important concepts introduced in this lesson include the idea of uploading a file. When we upload a file we put it on an Internet server (a computer with a connection to the Internet). In this lesson, when students upload an image file they put it on the App Inventor server. By uploading the image, students can then use it in their app.

When we download a file, we copy it from a remote computer onto our own computer. For example, we get an image file from the Internet.

You don't need to be concerned about privacy as this image is linked to the student's login identity. No one else can see it.

Before the lesson

During this lesson, students will upload a photo or other electronic image to the computer. Students can use a self-portrait photo or any other image. You may want to include taking a photo as an activity within the lesson, or in a prior lesson. As an alternative, you could direct students to a suitable Internet file search activity. App Inventor recognises a limited set of image formats. JPEG is a good choice. The interesting fact given for this lesson explains the JPEG format.

The key words for this lesson are: multimedia and upload. The words are highlighted in the text the first time they appear. Their definitions are included in the Key words box at the end of the lesson. You may want to review these words before the lesson.

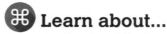 Learn about...

You will lead the first part of the lesson. Make sure students understand these ideas. You may ask them to make notes. You may use directed questioning to check understanding.

- **Multimedia content:** Explain what multimedia content is and why it can be an improvement on plain text. This could be a discussion topic. Why should we include images, sound and video in our apps?
- **Image formats:** You can review image formats. The three-letter extension at the end of a file name tells you the image format. Images should use the JPEG (.jpg) file format. You can load an image into Microsoft Paint and use the Save As option to convert images into JPEG format.
- **Prepare an image:** Explain how students can find suitable image files. If this material is already available, explain how to access it.

How to...

In the second part of the lesson students will complete an exercise under your guidance.

- **Locate an image:** Students find an image on the Internet, or take a photo, or find a photo they took earlier. They convert the image format to JPEG, if necessary.
- **Upload the image file:** Students upload the image file to the interface. Now the image is ready to use.
- **Add an image object to the interface:** Students add an image object. At this stage, the object does not show an image.
- **Set object properties:** Students change the properties of the image object. Change the Picture property to the uploaded image file. Change the Visible property to 'false'.

- **Add code:** Students add code blocks so that the image becomes visible when the ID button is pressed. The Student Book gives full instructions.

Now you do it...

Students amend the ID app so it shows a photo as well as a name. Students run the app and check that it works.

What success looks like: The interface and code will look similar to what is shown in the Student Book. The app will run and the image will appear when the user clicks on the button.

If you have time...

The extension activity gives students the opportunity to explore independently. The challenge is to add code so that the picture disappears when the Reset button is pressed. The Student Book has some tips.

What success looks like: The finished reset button code will look like this.

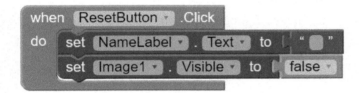

Test yourself...

FOUNDATION QUESTIONS

1 What is the event that makes the image visible? Answer: Clicking on the ID button.

2 What is the advantage of showing an image on an ID card? What else could you include on an ID card? Answer: An image makes the ID card more secure because it gives extra confirmation of your identity that can be checked. It helps to prove who you are. Some ID cards include descriptive text (e.g. height or hair colour). Some include other information such as your role, date of birth, and an ID number.

EXTENSION QUESTIONS

3 You added an image object to the interface. What is the purpose of this object? Answer: The image object links the photo file to the interface. So, this object will display the image on the interface.

4 You changed two properties of the image object. Why did you have to change these properties? Answer: You changed the image property to link the object to the right photo. You changed the Visible property to 'false' so the photo would not appear when the app is first started.

Learning outcomes

When they have completed this lesson students should be able to:

↗ design an interface with text boxes

↗ use logical tests and the `if` command to control the computer.

More-confident students will:

↗ attempt a longer activity that will review all skills learned to date.

Overview

Students will protect their ID card with a password. The ID card will only display students' identity if they enter the right password. This lesson introduces a key programming concept: using a logical test to change the behaviour of the computer. This is the most challenging lesson of this chapter. If necessary, you may need to use more than one lesson for this work.

Language development

Logical test is a technical term that is fully explained in the Student Book. The English word if has a technical meaning. The word if is used in programming to show a choice. If the test is 'true', then the computer follows the coded instructions.

Before the lesson

The key words for this lesson are: logical test. The words are highlighted in the text the first time they appear. The definition is included in the Key words box at the end of the lesson. You may want to review these words before the lesson.

Learn about...

You will lead the first part of the lesson. Make sure students understand these ideas. You may ask them to make notes. You may use directed questioning to check understanding.

- **Password:** Explain why we use passwords and the features of a good password. List examples where we use passwords and pass codes in everyday life.

- **Logical test:** A logical test is a test that can be 'true' or 'false'. We use logical tests to control the action of the computer. If the test is 'true' the computer does one thing, if the test is 'false' it does another.

- **Equals sign:** We compare two values in a logical test. The simplest comparison is the equals sign.

The test that uses the equals sign is 'true' if the two values are exactly the same. Otherwise, the test is 'false'.

Question for students to consider: What logical test will we use for a password check? Answer: we will test that the password entered by the user is equal to the right password. The right password is stored inside the computer.

Talk about...

What makes a good password? A good password must be easy to remember, but hard to guess. Should we change our passwords often? Should we write them down?

Ⓞ How to...

In the second part of the lesson students complete an exercise under your guidance.

- **Add password box:** Students will add a new box to the interface, where the user can type the password. Normally we use a text box to enter data on the screen of the computer. However, App Inventor offers a special password box. The password box lets you enter text, but does not show the letters you type. Students can add an ordinary text box to the interface, or a password text box.

- **Add a logical test:** Adding a logical test is a long and complex task. Students will use the yellow `if` block. Students will have to fit several different blocks together. You should take this activity slowly. Demonstrate each step clearly. Students must understand the purpose of each block.

- **Add code controlled by the logical test:** Finally, students take their existing blocks apart, and reassemble them, including the `if` block they just made. Once again, go slowly so that all students can follow the activity.

Now you do it...

Students follow your instructions, adding a password box and code to protect their ID card.

What success looks like: The Student Book shows the appearance of the interface and the completed code.

 # If you have time...

There are two extension activities. Students can add additional code, so that the Reset button clears the password box. This is a fairly short extension activity.

What success looks like: The completed Reset button code should look like this.

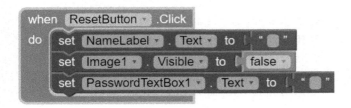

Students who are making good progress can try a larger activity which will review all skills learned to date. Students add a second button to the ID card app so they can display two different IDs. The interface will need a second button. If a user presses this button, a different name and image will appear on the interface. The second ID may also have a different password. This task can only be completed by students who have learned all the skills of previous lessons.

What success looks like: Students will be able to demonstrate an app with two ID buttons, each of which shows a different name and picture. A student who does not reach this standard should still get credit for whatever progress they have managed, and for working independently. Successful code may look something like this.

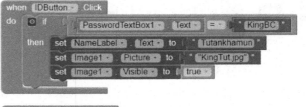

 # Test yourself...

FOUNDATION QUESTIONS

1 When you type letters into a password text box, the letters do not appear on the screen. Instead you see this symbol *. Why is that? Answer: This is to stop people seeing your password as you enter it, for example, by looking over your shoulder.

2 A logical test only has two possible answers. What are they? Answer: Logical tests have only two outcomes: 'true' or 'false'.

EXTENSION QUESTIONS

3 In this lesson there are three examples of tests that might be needed by software that runs a self-drive car. Think of some more tests that might be needed by this software. Answer: There is a range of possible answers. For example, a self-drive car needs to check that it is driving towards the set destination. The car needs to check it is keeping within the boundaries of the road and lane. It needs to stop if a pedestrian steps into the road. All of these actions are controlled by logical tests: they are either 'true' or 'false'.

4 Describe the logical test you used in this lesson. When is the result of the test 'true'? Answer: The logical test checked whether the text entered in the text box was equal to the word you chose as a password.

Learning outcomes

When they have completed this lesson students should be able to:

↗ test and evaluate a program to see whether it meets user needs.

More-confident students will:

↗ carry out additional tests

↗ add extra features to the program, without support.

Overview

Students have now completed the app. In the final lesson, they will test the app and record the results of their tests. You may ask students to test any future software solutions they develop, once it is clear they have the necessary skills.

Language development

Evaluate has a specific meaning in the context of any development project, including app development. Evaluate means ensuring that the project meets the client's requirements. Programmers must evaluate any product before it is released to the client. The client is the person who commissioned the project, will pay for the product, and has final approval over its functionality.

Before the lesson

Support students who have not managed to create a working app. As an alternative, you might give them access to a working version of the app to test in this lesson. However, all students should have at least a basic working ID card app by this stage.

The key words for this lesson are: client and evaluate. The words are highlighted in the text the first time they appear. Their definitions are included in the Key words box at the end of the lesson. You may want to review these words before the lesson.

⌘ Learn about...

You will lead the first part of the lesson. Make sure students understand these ideas. You may ask them to make notes. You may use directed questioning to check understanding.

- **Evaluation:** Put software development into the wider context—the programmer makes a product for a real-life client. When you work as a programmer, you must test your software before you give it to the client. Does the software do what it is supposed to do?

- **Testing:** Testing is a methodical process intended to uncover any remaining problems with the software, so they can be fixed.

- **Software development:** Software is developed in a structured process called the 'development lifecycle'. Testing and evaluation are an essential part of development.

- **Improvement:** The purpose of the testing and evaluation stages is to improve the software. This improvement can continue after the software is released. Companies often release new versions of apps, with improvements.

💬 Talk about...

Discuss the features that might be added to an ID card app to improve it. For example, the ID card might play a sample of your voice, or include a fingerprint image. Students can be imaginative in suggesting possible features.

⏻ How to...

In the second part of the lesson students complete an exercise under your guidance.

- **Test plan:** Programmers must plan tests and record the results in a structured form. It is important to test every aspect of the software. Students may use a word-processing application (such as Microsoft Word) which has a table feature. Help them to create a table with all the right columns and rows, such as the one in the Student Book on page 58.

- **Carry out tests:** Now students load the app, and carry out the four planned tests. They must record the results in the test table.

- **Analyse test results:** Finally, the app is closed and students look at the completed test table.

Now you do it...

Students make a test plan, carry out tests on the program and record test results.

What success looks like: Students have a completed test table showing the results of their test, and have thoroughly evaluated their app.

 If you have time...

More able students can devise and carry out extra tests. Students who are far ahead of their classmates may improve their app by adding extra features. There are App Inventor teaching materials online, which are student friendly. Encourage highly confident students to extend their learning.

What success looks like: Students have extended their learning by carrying out extra tests or adding extra features to their app.

 Test yourself...

FOUNDATION QUESTIONS

1 Why does a programmer evaluate a program? Answer: A programmer evaluates a program to check whether it meets the client's requirements.

2 What is test data? Answer: Test data is the input that we enter into the app when we run a test.

EXTENSION QUESTIONS

3 A programmer made a test plan. One column of the plan was called 'Expected Result'. What goes in that column? Answer: The expected result column shows what output the app should produce, if it is working properly and doing what the client expects.

4 A programmer tested an app. Analysis of test results showed that the programmer had more work to do before the app was ready. Explain why. Answer: If the test results do not match the expected results, then there is more work to do. The programmer must improve the app until the output exactly matches the client's requirements.

The test questions and assessment activities give you an opportunity to evaluate students' understanding. The questions are shown here with possible answers.

Model answers to test questions

1   A touch-screen interface is made up of objects. Describe three objects you can add to a touch-screen interface. Answer: These are the objects students have used in this chapter: Button, Label, Text box (or Password text box) and Image. Most students will pick three from this list. There are other touch-screen objects, which advanced students may pick. If in doubt, check the palette of objects on the App Inventor design screen.

2   The objects on an interface have properties. Describe three properties of interface objects. Answer: There are several properties including Colour, Text, Size, Picture and Visible. Most students will pick three from this list. There are other properties, which advanced students may pick. If in doubt, check the object properties section on the App Inventor design screen.

3   What is a client? Answer: A full answer may cover these points: A client is the person who has paid for the software application (app) to be made. The app must meet client needs. Clients sign-off the project when they are happy with it. Give marks if the student understands that the client is the person whose needs must be met when making and finalising the app.

4   Explain why you must know the client's requirements before you begin making an app. Answer: The app should meet the client's requirements. You need to know what those requirements are before you begin making the app.

5   App Inventor is an event-driven visual programming language. Explain what that means. Answer: Students should define 'event-driven programming': The commands in the program are only carried out when an event happens. Students should define 'visual programming': the program code is made of visual elements (coloured blocks) which fit together. Extra credit if students say: The event is called a trigger. In the ID card app, the trigger is to touch a button on the interface screen.

6   What is a logical test? Answer: A logical test is a test that has the answer 'true' or 'false'. Extra credit: A typical logical test compares two values.

7   Explain how the equals sign is used in a logical test. Answer: The equals sign compares two values to see if they are exactly the same. If they are the same, the test is 'true'.

The next three questions relate to this image. The image shows a block of program code. The code is part of a science quiz.

8   What is the logical test in this block of code? Answer: It tests whether the text in AnswerBox is the same as the word Mammal.

9   What happens if the result of the logical test is 'true'? Answer: If the test is 'true', a label called ResultLabel shows the sentence, 'Your answer is right'.

10 What event triggers this block of code? Answer: The block of code is triggered when the user clicks a button called CheckAnswerButton.

Model answers to assessment activities

Starter activity

All students should be able to complete this activity. Students only have to copy **exactly** what they see in the Student Book. The student must drag four buttons, one label, and one image object onto the Viewer screen and relabel them as shown here.

What success looks like: The interface the student makes should have four buttons, a label and an image object. It does not need to look exactly like the picture, but it should have the features. The student must find a picture of Machu Picchu online and upload it as media content for the app. The student must then make this block of code.

In this example, we have called the photo Peru.jpg. Substitute the name of the student's photo. Apart from the photo name, the code should look exactly like this example.

When the student runs the app they should be able to press the Machu Picchu button and see the photo they uploaded.

Intermediate activity

This activity is similar to the Starter activity. However, students will have to find and upload photos of all the landmarks mentioned in the app. Students will then add code to each button so that when the user clicks a button, a suitable photo and message appears.

A quick way to do this is to right-click the code for Machu Picchu and choose Duplicate from the menu. Change the name at the top of the Duplicate block from MachuButton to AyersButton. Change the text and the name of the image, and the background colour. Now the code works perfectly for the second button.

Repeat this until you have code for all four buttons.

Extension activity

There are three extension activities for confident students. Students can complete these unassisted as all the Student Book has all the guidance they will need. You can concentrate on supporting students that need more help.

- **Add password protection and a Reset button:** Students can base this on their activity in Lesson 2.5 (Password protection).

- **Test the app and record test results:** Student can base their testing on what they learned in Lesson 2.6 (Test and evaluate).

- **Add extra features:** If students finish before their classmates, they can explore adding new features to the app. For example, they could add more text about each famous landmark, or they could add extra landmarks. They could improve the appearance of the interface.

What success looks like: Ask students to describe and show the working app. Give credit for any successful working features. Even if the work is not 100 per cent successful, give credit to students who explore and work independently.

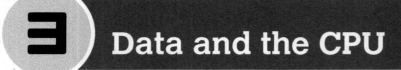
Curriculum coverage

This chapter covers part or all of the requirements for the Computing Programme of Study (age 11–14):

↗ understand how numbers can be represented in binary

↗ be able to carry out simple operations on binary numbers [conversion between binary and decimal].

This chapter also covers these main requirements for the Computing at School (CAS) Progression Pathways (for a full list of requirements met, see pages 9–10 of this handbook):

↗ know that digital computers use binary to represent all data

↗ know that computers transfer data in binary

↗ distinguish between data used in a simple program (a variable) and the storage structure for that data.

Preparation

There is no requirement for special software in this chapter. Most of the computer-based activity involves searching the Internet. Finding some relevant websites that you can point students to if their web search skills are less well developed may help lessons run more smoothly. For example, in Lesson 3.1 students consider the use of microprocessors in everyday devices, such as washing machines. Many websites include examples of everyday use of microprocessors at a suitable level. Using the search string 'Microprocessors in everyday life' will find some example sites you can choose from.

In Lesson 3.6, students use ASCII code. You could search for a suitable ASCII table that students can use during the lesson. If you have the resources, you can print some copies out for students to use. Otherwise, you can display the code on the board or provide a web link if students have a computer available. The example you choose should include only the 128 basic ASCII characters and the binary version of the code. Not all ASCII tables contain these specific items.

The more students practise converting between decimal and binary, the more confident they will get. There are many opportunities for them to practise in the lesson. However, you may want to prepare some additional exercises to use with advanced students and those requiring additional support.

Learning outcomes

By completing this chapter students will be able to:

- explain why computers use binary code
- convert decimal numbers into binary
- convert binary numbers into decimal
- explain how counting works in decimal and binary
- explain how computers use binary numbers to store useful information such as text and symbols
- explain why a computer needs to use code to communicate
- encode and decode simple messages
- show that simple programs use variables and constants
- explain that the data are stored in a data structure.

Sending codes

Talk about...

The discussion is an activity you can do offline. You could use this activity any time to vary the pace of lessons and encourage students to reflect on their learning.

The discussion in this lesson asks students to think about where microprocessors are used in everyday life. Encourage them to draw from their own experience. That experience can be in the home, in school and also in the wider world. They will, for example, come across many uses in retail settings and as they travel around in a car. The modern car is full of microprocessor-controlled functions from engine monitoring to satellite navigation and climate control.

###

This fact tells students a little about the history of using coded messages. The chapter covers Morse and ASCII codes and students are told that they will be sending some coded messages later in the chapter.

Two other Fact boxes appear in the chapter (Microprocessors in Lesson 3.1 and Nibbles and bytes in Lesson 3.6.) These are points of interest for students and could be useful topics for discussion.

Word cloud

The Word cloud contains all the key words that have been highlighted and defined in Key words boxes throughout the lesson. The key words for this chapter are: ASCII code, unicode, binary, clock speed, microprocessor, bit, binary digit, byte, decimal digit, carry, cipher, Morse code.

Learning outcomes

When they have completed this lesson students should be able to:

↗ explain why computers use binary code.

More-confident students will:

↗ change object properties and evaluate the effect of these changes.

Overview

This lesson defines a computer. The lesson identifies the microprocessor as being the brain of the computer. As microprocessors have become smaller, they have been built into many devices such as mobile phones, cars and household appliances. The lesson describes the basic two states of switches in a microprocessor. This architecture is used to explain why a computer must use binary as its language.

Before the lesson

Prepare an introduction to the learning activities ('**Now you do it...** ' and '**If you have time...** ') to identify microprocessors. If possible, use local examples of devices that use microprocessors to start the student discussion. For example, has the school had new equipment installed? The school might have a new access control, such as a key card system or perhaps your library has an automated way of tracking books. Maybe there is a new high-profile development in your local town or city that students will recognise. For example, a new road development might have computer-controlled signage to manage traffic flow. A new cinema complex might have computer-controlled LED advertising displays or an interactive self-service ticket kiosk.

The key words for this lesson are: binary, clock speed and microprocessor. The words are highlighted when they first appear in the text. Their definitions are included in the Key words box at the end of the lesson. You may want to review these words before the lesson.

⌘ Learn about...

You will lead the first part of the lesson. Make sure students understand these ideas. You may ask them to make notes. You may use directed questioning to check understanding.

- **Central Processing Unit (CPU):** The CPU is the computer's brain. At the centre of the CPU is a microprocessor. Microprocessors have become smaller and more powerful over time. We now carry computers in a pocket. These computers are more powerful than those of 60 years ago, that would have filled a room.
- **Clock speed:** A computer works by carrying out small instructions. It carries out an instruction each time its clock ticks. The speed of the clock is partly responsible for the speed of the computer.
- **Two-state architecture:** A microprocessor is made up of millions of switches. Each switch can be 'on' or 'off'. The term 'two-state' architecture isn't introduced in the Student Book. However, students should understand that computers use binary code because the two digits used match the on–off state of its switches.

How to...

In the second part of the lesson students complete an exercise under your guidance.

Clock speed: This exercise shows how fast the computer can carry out instructions compared with humans. Most people believe that computers carry out complicated instructions. In fact, computers carry out simple instructions quickly. It will be helpful to emphasise this in your summary of the activity.

Now you do it...

You can choose whether to have students complete this activity individually or in small groups. You could include a challenge to see which individual student or group can come up with the longest list of devices. Whichever approach you choose, students will benefit from a class session at the end to bring the results together.

What success looks like: Students' answers may include:

- **computers and computer-related devices:** desktop computers, laptops, phones, games consoles
- **entertainment devices:** televisions, digital radios, mp3 players, dvd players, on-demand video consoles
- **appliances:** washing machines, ovens, microwave oven (anything with digital readout and programmes)
- **utilities:** electricity or gas meters, alarm systems.

 If you have time...

This activity asks students to think about which actions microprocessors control in a particular device: the washing machine.

What success looks like: Students' answers may include: Open/close valves to let water in and out; the length of the wash cycle; the temperature of water; the temperature of the air in the drying cycle; the spin speed; safety cut-out if device overheats or blockage occurs; the door lock.

 Test yourself...

FOUNDATION QUESTIONS

1 What is the language used by computers called?
Answer: The computer's language is binary.

2 What does 'micro' in microprocessor mean?
Answer: Micro means very small.

EXTENSION QUESTIONS

3 Why does a computer have a clock? Answer: The computer clock co-ordinates the activity of a computer. Each time the clock ticks, the computer carries out an instruction.

4 What does 'giga' in gigahertz mean? Answer: Giga means one thousand million. A one gigahertz clock pulses one thousand million times per second.

Learning outcomes

When they have completed this lesson students should be able to:

↗ convert binary numbers into decimal.

More-confident students will:

↗ demonstrate an understanding of conversion between base 2 and base 10 by applying the principles to another number base.

Overview

In this lesson students will develop their understanding of binary. They will learn what base 10 and base 2 mean for:

- the number of digits used in a number system
- the value assigned to each column for a number in a value table.

Students will use this information to convert binary digits to decimal numbers. The lesson also defines the terms bit and byte.

Language development

Two important technical terms used in this lesson are bit and byte. In the world of computing, a bit is a single binary digit. The word bit comes from the first and last two letters of **b**inary dig**it**. Bit has other English language uses. A bit is a small amount. Bit is also the past tense of the verb 'bite'. To bite means to cut into with the teeth. The word byte (spelled with a 'y') is a technical term used to describe a group of eight binary digits.

Before the lesson

Prepare some further examples of binary numbers to convert for those students who progress well or who need additional practice during the lesson. All students will benefit from more practice when learning this new skill. The key words for this lesson are: bit, binary digit, byte and decimal digit. The words are highlighted in the text. Their definitions are included in the Key words box at the end of the lesson. You may want to review these words before the lesson.

⌘ Learn about...

You will lead the first part of the lesson. Make sure students understand these ideas. You may ask them to make notes. You may use directed questioning to check understanding.

The lesson introduces base 10 and base 2. These terms make it easier to remember the number of different, unique digits used in a number system. These terms also make it easier to remember the value of the columns of a number in a value table. Students learn to convert binary to decimal by following these steps:

1 Create a value table with decimal headings, like this one.

	64	32	16	8	4	2	1

2 Enter the number to be converted into the table.

128	64	32	16	8	4	2	1
0	0	1	1	0	0	1	0

3 Add together the decimal values from the table heading for each column where a '1' occurs in the binary number:

$$32 + 16 + 2 = 50$$

How to...

In the second part of the lesson students complete an exercise under your guidance.

Students learn the technique for converting a binary number into decimal described in the '**Learn about...** ' section. Students should lay out the conversion in a table. Doing this will support students as they develop their understanding. It will also help you and students resolve errors.

Students should calculate the column values, rather than learn them by rote. More able students should extend this skill so that they are able to calculate column values of a two-byte number. They will be asked to do this later, in the Lesson 3.3 extension activity ('**If you have time...** ').

In *Matrix* Student Books 2 and 3, students will go on to learn how images can be represented by groups of three bytes. Students need a firm understanding of binary and the concepts of different number systems. Learning to calculate the column values now will help them grasp more advanced concepts later.

The Student Book asks students to express binary numbers in byte form—as eight-bit numbers. For example, 1011 is expressed as 00001011.

 Now you do it...

It will be helpful to introduce this activity with a review of how to convert binary numbers to decimal. Recap the rules of the game so all students understand the task. If you put students into larger groups, or have an odd number of students, state clearly how they should pass the sheets. Everyone passes their sheet to the right, for example. Take time to help those students who are not yet confident with binary conversion.

What success looks like: Students convert three bytes of binary to decimal.

 If you have time...

This activity will challenge the more advanced students in your class. The activity asks them to apply the principles they used when learning about base 2 and base 10 to a new situation. This activity asks them to convert from base 6 to decimal.

What success looks like: The answer to the challenge is: 53 (36 + 12 + 5)

	36	6	1
	1	2	5
Decimal	36	12	5

 Test yourself...

FOUNDATION QUESTIONS

1 Convert the binary value 1101 into a decimal. Answer: 13

2 What is each of the digits in a byte called? Answer: Each digit is called a bit. The word bit stands for binary digit.

EXTENSION QUESTIONS

3 How would you write 100111 as a byte? Answer: 0100111 (a leading zero is added to make the number of digits up to eight).

4 What is the largest number that can be stored in a byte? Give your answer in binary and decimal. Answer: In binary the largest number is 11111111. That is 255 in decimal.

Learning outcomes

When they have completed this lesson students should be able to:

↗ convert decimal numbers into binary

↗ explain how computers use binary numbers.

More-confident students will:

↗ apply the knowledge they have learned about binary conversion to larger two-byte numbers.

Overview

In this lesson students will learn how to convert decimal numbers into binary using the 'descending powers of two and subtraction' method. They are not taught the name of the technique. The name of the technique is provided here so you can do your own research in preparation for the lesson, if you want. Students are also taught that larger binary numbers can be stored by using more than one byte.

Before the lesson

Prepare some decimal to binary conversion questions, in addition to those in the lesson. You may want to use these questions with those students who progress well or who need additional practice during the lesson. Limit your examples to decimal values between 1 and 255 so that the answer will fit into a single byte. All students will benefit from practice when learning this new skill.

Your students may have already carried out decimal to binary conversion in a Maths lesson. Check with the Maths department to find out what technique they may have used. This lesson uses a technique called 'descending powers of two and subtraction'. There is another method called 'short division by two with remainder'. It is best to proceed with the method used in the *Matrix* book. You will need to explain the *Matrix* method as an alternative if students have previously used another method.

⌘ Learn about...

You will lead the first part of the lesson. Preparing one or two examples to use in an introduction to this part of the lesson will be helpful to students.

As with binary to decimal conversion in Lesson 3.2, stress the need for students to lay out their work neatly. They should also show all their workings.

This will help their understanding of the process and make it easier to correct errors.

In the second part of the lesson students will be asked to think about what the biggest number a byte can hold is. This question can lead you and students into discussing the need to use multiple bytes to store larger numbers. There is no need to introduce the concept of overflow and the errors that might arise from it at this stage in students' learning.

⏻ How to...

The second part of the lesson will involve students carrying out a learning activity, under your guidance.

Use your introduction to the '**Learn about...**' section to demonstrate the technique of converting from decimal to binary to students. If you have time, use two examples. Use the first example as a demonstration. Take the opportunity to involve students through questions and answers in solving the second example. This will lead them into the independent activity in the '**Now you do it...**' section of the Student Book.

⊕ Now you do it...

Students are asked to convert decimal numbers into binary using the technique shown. When you introduce the activity, explain that they should show their working. Demonstrate an example on the board before they start the activity, if you have the time.

What success looks like: The answers to the three questions are:

- 79 = 01001111
- 138 = 10001010
- 225 = 11100001

If you have time...

This extension activity asks students to convert larger decimal numbers into binary. Two of the numbers in the activity will occupy two bytes. There are two parts to this activity. First, students will have to calculate the column values for each bit in the second byte. Second, they convert the decimal values into two-byte binary. Students may use a calculator for this activity.

What success looks like: The answers to the three questions are:

- 255 = 00000000 11111111
- 1455 = 00000101 10101111
- 5100 = 00010011 11101100

 Test yourself...

FOUNDATION QUESTIONS

1 What What would 0 look like if written as a byte? Answer: 00000000—a byte is always expressed as eight bits so must contain leading zeros.

2 How many bits are there in two bytes? Answer: 16 (8 × 2).

EXTENSION QUESTIONS

3 The largest decimal number that can be stored in two bytes is 65,535. What would you do to store a larger number than that? Answer: Use a third byte to store the number. It would be incorrect to say use an extra bit—the computer will always use a full byte.

4 How can you tell whether a binary number is odd or even? Answer: If the digit to the extreme right of the binary number is a 0, the number is even. If it is 1, then number is odd.

Overview

In this lesson students will learn how to count in binary. In decimal we have names for every number. Those decimal names help us communicate number information to each other. Using the names of numbers also help us when we learn to count as young children. Students will all be able to count in decimal without thinking about it. However, they might find it more difficult to explain the process of counting.

There are no names for individual binary numbers. We use terms such as kilobyte, megabyte and gigabyte to communicate information about binary values. However, 00110000 has no name. When we communicate detailed number information about binary, we convert the value and use its decimal name. We cannot learn to count in binary by chanting the names of numbers as we do in decimal. To learn to count in binary, students will have to understand the process of counting. This lesson will develop that understanding.

Before the lesson

Read through the activity that asks students to make a binary counting machine out of squares of paper. Run through the activity yourself so that you can demonstrate the principles confidently when you introduce the lesson.

Prepare a version of the binary counting machine so you can show how it works when you introduce the activity. To do this, you might create a PowerPoint demonstration which steps through the first three numbers in the count on separate slides. As an alternative, you could create a template to project onto the board and use marker pens to demonstrate each step.

If you have a visualiser, you could build the machine as described in the text and project it onto the board to demonstrate. Whatever you choose, make sure the rules are visible so you can refer to them as you proceed through the demonstration.

You will need to provide sheets of paper or card, scissors and rulers so that students can build the machine during the lesson.

The key word for this lesson is: carry. This key word is highlighted the first time it appears in the text. The definition is included in the Key words box at the end of the lesson. You may want to review the meaning of this word before the lesson.

⌘ Learn about...

You will lead the first part of the lesson. Make sure students understand these ideas. You may ask them to make notes. You may use directed questioning to check understanding.

Take the opportunity to review number bases. Students must understand these points.

- In the base-2 number system, there are two digits: 0 and 1.
- As you move from right to left, the value of each column in a value table is two times greater than the previous one.

The principle of 'carrying' during counting is central. Demonstrate carrying using decimal and binary examples, before students move on to independent activity.

⏻ How to...

In the second part of the lesson students complete an exercise under your guidance.

Prepare and present an introduction to the binary counting machine activity used in this lesson. Students often find it difficult to follow a list of rules. Therefore, it will be helpful if you have explained the first three steps of the binary count (from 000 to 011) during your introduction.

Make your demonstration as interactive as possible. Challenge the class to describe each step before you carry it out on the board. You might have your class build their binary count engines before you start your introduction so they can follow your demonstration using their own machine.

Now you do it...

Students will work in small groups to demonstrate how counting in binary works. If they use the rules written in the activity, they will be able to operate the counter correctly. Run through the first two or three counts on the board before asking students to carry out the activity themselves. Make sure you understand the counting machine and the rules for using it so you can help less confident students.

What success looks like: Students make and use a counting machine to count in binary from 1 to 7.

Set a new challenge for those students who have progressed confidently with the task. Ask those students to extend the binary counting machine to five digits. They are to think of a decimal number between 10 and 25. They should set up that number in the digits of their counting machine. They then count up five from that starting position, using the same rules they used to count from zero. Students record the result of each count in binary. They can then check their work by converting their results to decimal at the end of the activity.

If you have time...

This is the final lesson on binary maths. Students are asked to review Lessons 3.1 to 3.4 to make sure they understand the content before moving on. You can redirect more-able students to the activities in Lessons 3.2 and 3.3, where students can set each other challenges. Further practise in converting between decimal and binary will improve their confidence.

What success looks like: Students review their learning until they are confident with all the material in the chapter so far.

Test yourself...

FOUNDATION QUESTIONS

1 When do you know a single count (e.g. from 00000111 to 00001000) is completed? Answer: You know it is completed when a binary digit that is 0 changes to 1.

2 If you count one step from 0000001, what happens in the units column? Answer: The units column is set to 0.

EXTENSION QUESTIONS

3 Why do you carry more often in binary than in decimal? Answer: Each binary digit only has two possible values. That means the bit reaches its highest value and causes a carry more often than in a decimal digit, which has nine possible values.

4 Why don't you use words such as 'seven', 'eight' and 'nine' when you count in binary? Answer: Seven, eight and nine are words used in decimal counting. There are no equivalents in binary. If we say 0000111 is 'seven', we are actually converting to decimal.

Learning outcomes

When they have completed this lesson students should be able to:

↗ explain why a computer needs to use code to communicate

↗ encode and decode simple messages.

More-confident students will:

↗ research and use a code of their choice to communicate.

Overview

Computers store and process all data in binary. A computer is useful when it can receive data from humans and provide information in a form that humans can understand. To do this, the computer uses codes that allow its binary data to be output as words, images and sound.

This lesson introduces the idea of codes. It explores the way humans use codes and ciphers to translate messages into a form that others cannot easily read. We use codes for security reasons. We use codes to make communicating our information harder for those we don't want to see it. The computer uses codes for the opposite reason, to make communication easier. This idea is developed in Lesson 3.6, where students will learn about ASCII code.

Language development

In English language the words code and cipher are often used to mean the same thing: A method of writing a secret message. In fact they have slightly different meanings. A code is where one symbol is randomly chosen to represent another. So, in Morse code three dashes represent the letter 'O'. There is no logical pattern for what symbol is chosen.

A cipher also substitutes one symbol for another in a message. The difference is that a cipher uses an algorithm to decide which symbol is used to replace another. So, in the Caesar cipher we count three steps along the alphabet to find the replacement symbol. A becomes D, and so on. You can decipher a message if you know the algorithm.

The word cipher came into the English language from Arabic. *Sifr* is the Arabic pronunciation for the number zero.

Before the lesson

This lesson uses the Caesar cipher and some variations, as a basis for student activities. Make sure you understand the Caesar cipher before the lesson, so you can support students during the activities. Consider using a Caesar cipher wheel to make the coding and decoding easier for students. You can find templates online for this wheel, using a web search for 'Caesar cipher wheel template'. It is not advisable to take time creating a wheel yourself for the limited activity in this lesson. However, you should consider creating a wheel for the Intermediate activity in the Review section at the end of the chapter.

The '**How to...**' section challenges students to learn about Morse code and send a short message to another student. Consider a practical method they can use to send their messages. The Student Book makes some suggestions, but you can choose a method yourself. Agree the method with students during the introduction to the lesson. A copy of Morse code is included in the Student Book (page 82). You could download a copy from the Internet and project it onto the board during the Morse code activity.

In the '**If you have time...**' activity, students will use a web search to investigate other codes that can be used. Investigate alternative codes yourself before the lesson. Choose one or two that you can recommend to students to try for themselves. Braille and pigpen are codes that are often used as examples.

The key words for this lesson are cipher and Morse code. Their definitions are included in the Key words box at the end of the lesson. You may want to review these words before the lesson.

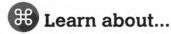 Learn about...

You will lead the first part of the lesson. Make sure students understand these ideas. You may ask them to make notes. You may use directed questioning to check understanding.

- **Why do humans use codes?** Codes add security to messages. Codes make it hard for unauthorised people to read messages. An example is personal data sent by people to banks. That data are coded when sent across the Internet, so they can't be easily intercepted and read.

- **Why do computers use codes?** Computers use codes because the computer's language (binary) is different from our own. The computer uses codes to translate binary into a form people can understand. However, computers also use codes for the same reason as people: to keep data secure.

- **Code example 1, Caesar cipher:** Caesar cipher is an example of a code used to make information secret and secure. Only someone who knows the key to the code can decipher and read it.

- **Code example 2, Morse code:** Morse is an example of a code used to translate between different 'languages'. In this case, the conversion is between human communication and pulses of electricity sent along a telegraph wire. There are many similarities between Morse code and ASCII code.

How to...

In the second part of the lesson students complete an exercise under your guidance.

Students will work in pairs to send messages to each other using the Caesar cipher and Morse code.

- **Caesar cipher:** Stress the importance of clarity in laying out the code so that students' partners can successfully decipher the message. Discourage students from writing long messages as that will waste valuable time. Set a character limit on messages.

- **Morse code:** Agree a method of signalling dots and dashes with your class during the introduction to the activity. For example, students could hold up a closed hand and signal dots and dashes by opening their hand for a long or short period.

 Now you do it...

Students create a code where they substitute letters for binary numbers. In the first part of the activity, students create their code by completing a table. The table assigns a number to each lower-case letter in the alphabet and a limited number of punctuation characters. If you want to reduce the time required for this activity, you can prepare a completed code sheet in advance. Introduce the activity and stress that students should write short questions. For example, "How old are you?" In this activity and the **'If you have time...'** extension activity, students should work in pairs. Larger groups can be used if you instruct group members to pass their messages and ciphers to the person on the right.

What success looks like: Students successfully code and decode each other's messages.

 If you have time...

Students search the Internet for other examples of ciphers and codes. You may want to find some examples before the lesson so you can guide students who are struggling to find a good example. The pigpen code and Braille are suggestions you could use to help a student focus their search more effectively.

What success looks like: Students research and find codes to use to communicate.

Test yourself...

FOUNDATION QUESTIONS

1 What is the Caesar cipher? Answer: Caesar cipher is a code that shifts each letter in the alphabet three characters to the right. For example, A becomes D.

2 Why does a computer need to use codes to communicate with people? Answer: A computer uses code to translate between binary and language humans can understand. ASCII code is used to convert the binary numbers that a computer stores and processes into letters that humans can read.

EXTENSION QUESTIONS

3 Explain how Morse code is similar to binary code. Answer: A binary digit can be in one of two states—one or zero. Morse code is made up of two signals—dots and dashes.

4 What is a key used for in codes? Answer: A key unlocks a code. The key tells the receiver how to decode a message.

Learning outcomes

When they have completed this lesson students should be able to:

↗ explain how computers use binary numbers to store useful information such as text and symbols.

More-confident students will:

↗ use an ASCII table to convert text to its binary equivalent.

Overview

Students will apply their knowledge of codes to the computer's use of ASCII code. Computers use ASCII code to translate letters, numbers and other characters, such as punctuation marks, from human-readable form to binary. Once the characters are converted to binary, the computer can store and process them. Students will learn about the limitations of the 128-character ASCII code, which is unable to support any language other than English. The lesson also introduces Extended ASCII and Unicode.

Language development

ASCII stands for American Standard Code for Information Interchange. We usually say 'ASCII' and it has its own pronunciation: ask-ee. In English language, this is an acronym. An acronym is used as shorthand for a long phrase or name in both written and spoken English.

Computing uses many other acronyms. For example, LAN and WAN are acronyms for local and wide area networks. An abbreviation only becomes an acronym when it has a common pronunciation. Acronyms are always written in upper case.

Sometimes an acronym is in such common use that it becomes accepted as a word in its own right. Laser is an example of an acronym (light amplification by stimulated emission of radiation) that has now become a word. As a word, laser is written in lower case.

Before the lesson

Students are asked to create a full binary text table by extending fragments of the code that are included in the lesson text. More able students may do this quickly, but others may take a long time on this task. You could have copies of the ASCII table available to give to students if it is taking too long.

As an alternative to handouts, you could download an ASCII table from the Internet and create an abbreviated version that includes only upper-case and lower-case characters. You could project this table onto the board after students have had time to try to complete the lesson activity table themselves.

The key words for this lesson are: ASCII code and Unicode. The words are highlighted the first time they appear in the text. Their definitions are included in the Key words box at the end of the lesson. You may want to review these words before the lesson.

⌘ Learn about...

You will lead the first part of the lesson. Make sure students understand these ideas. You may ask them to make notes. You may use directed questioning to check understanding.

- **ASCII code:** ASCII is a code used by the computer to convert characters into binary code to be stored and processed. There are 128 ASCII characters including letters numbers, punctuation characters and control keys, such as the escape key (ESC). Only seven bits in the byte are used to store the characters. ASCII only supports English.

- **Extended ASCII code:** This uses the eighth bit to extend ASCII code to 255 characters. The additional characters include letters with accents that extend ASCII to include European languages other than English.

- **Unicode:** Unicode extends the character set that can be used to include hundreds of extra languages and scripts. Unicode uses up to four bytes to store characters. Unicode supports scripts, such as Arabic and Mandarin, allowing computers to be used in almost any language. Unicode is a more complex code than ASCII. ASCII is included in the Unicode character set, so the two are compatible.

How to...

In the second part of the lesson students complete an exercise under your guidance. Students investigate how the ASCII table is constructed. The Student Book provides fragments of ASCII code. Students are asked to extend those fragments to create a full list of characters and numbers. Guide students through this process in your introduction.

The tables in the Student Book provide the ASCII codes for the upper-case and lower-case characters A to C and Z. Work through a few letters to demonstrate how to extend the list. Use question and answer challenges as you demonstrate. There are two methods students can use to complete the table:

- use binary counting skills to add 1 to the code for each successive letter of the alphabet, or
- add 1 to the decimal code for each successive letter, then convert the decimal values into binary.

You should point out that students do not need to work out the codes for both upper-case and lower-case characters. If they have worked out that the ASCII code for D is 01000100, then they simply switch the sixth digit from 0 to 1 to get the lower-case character. Lower-case d is 01100100.

This activity will not only develop students' knowledge of ASCII and data representation, it will help them gain confidence in using binary numbers.

Now you do it...

In this activity students translate a message written in binary into English by using ASCII code. Students can complete this activity by using the fragments of ASCII code included in the body of the lesson. To do this, they will have to complete their own ASCII table for letters of the alphabet. To save time, you can provide them with a copy of the full ASCII code or a link to a suitable web page. Make sure the copy of the ASCII you provide includes the binary code.

What success looks like: The message in binary translates to: Binary is 100% fun!

All the characters required for this message are either in the lesson text or can be worked out by extending the partial tables that are provided.

If you have time...

This activity is similar to the '**Now you do it...**' learning activity. However, none of the characters in the message are included in the lesson text. Your students will need to find a suitable ASCII code table online to complete this activity. If you already provided an ASCII code table to simplify the main activity, you can substitute another web search for students carrying out this extension activity. For example, students can search the Internet for a binary to ASCII code converter.

What success looks like: The message in binary translates to: :-)

Test yourself...

FOUNDATION QUESTIONS

1 Why is ASCII code important when you press a key on your keyboard? Answer: When a key is pressed on a keyboard, ASCII code is used to translate the character on the key into a binary code.

2 How many characters are in the ASCII code? Answer: 128—Seven bits are used for the ASCII code.

EXTENSION QUESTIONS

3 What is the advantage of Unicode over ASCII? Answer: Unicode can store many more characters than ASCII. Unicode allows computers to be used in many languages, not just English.

4 Why can Unicode support so many characters (128,000)? Answer: Unicode uses up to four bytes to store characters. ASCII only uses one byte.

The test questions and assessment activities in the Student Book give you an opportunity to evaluate students' understanding. The questions are shown here with possible answers.

 ## Model answers to test questions

1   What is a binary number? Answer: Binary is also called base 2. That means a binary number only uses two digits, zero and one. Each column in a binary number is two times higher than the previous column.

2   How is the decimal 27 represented as a binary number? Answer: 00011011 (students should be writing numbers in full byte form.)

3   What is the name of a single binary digit? Answer: A bit is a single binary digit.

4   What is a byte? Answer: A byte is a group of eight bits.

5   What is the ASCII code for a character? Answer: An ASCII code is a binary number that is used by a computer to represent keyboard characters.

6   What do the letters CPU represent? Answer: The letters represent the words Central Processing Unit.

7   Why is clock speed important in a computer? Answer: Clock speed determines how quickly instructions can be carried out by a computer. The faster the clock speed the faster a computer will run.

8   What does a microprocessor do? Answer: A microprocessor is the brain of a computer. It receives instructions, carries them out and reports the results back to the user.

9   In what format do computers transfer data? Answer: Binary—computers do everything in binary.

10 How is the binary number 01001011 represented in decimal? Answer: 75.

✓ Model answers to assessment activities

Starter activity

Students demonstrate their understanding of binary to decimal conversion and the use of ASCII code to represent data. Students should present their ASCII table neatly in order to use it successfully in the second part of the activity. Stress the importance of accuracy and layout in your introduction to this activity. There is no need for students to create long messages to demonstrate success in the activity. You might want to put a character limit on messages in your introduction.

What success looks like: A successful student will have assigned the correct ASCII codes to the upper-case letters of the alphabet. The table will be laid out neatly so that it is easy to read. The student will use the table confidently when creating and decoding messages.

Intermediate activity

Students combine the knowledge they have gained about ASCII code with their skills in using code. The first part of the activity asks them to create a table that will allow them to substitute a letter for binary code. There is no reason why they should not use the ASCII table they developed in the Starter activity to save time.

In the second part of the activity, students develop code that uses a key. In your introduction to this activity, suggest they use a Caesar cipher. The key will indicate number of characters to shift characters to the right. Consider using a Caesar cipher wheel to make the coding and decoding easier for students. There are templates available online, search for 'Caesar cipher wheel template'. Asking students to create a wheel will take a little time at the start of the lesson, but it will save time in the activity. If both coder and decoder have a wheel, the only information that needs to be sent with the message is the code key. That is, an instruction to turn the wheel by x characters.

In the final part of the exercise, students work with a partner to code and decode messages. Use your introduction to stress that the messages need not be long. Set a character limit, if you want to.

What success looks like: Students create a code that works and can describe it clearly. The code instructions and character-to-binary table are be laid out neatly so that coding and decoding are easy to carry out.

Extension activity

Students create a presentation that explains the process of converting a decimal number into binary. If students have experience of using a presentation package such as PowerPoint, they should use it to create the presentation. Otherwise, they can use a word processor or graphics package. Suggest in your introduction that students limit their presentation to the conversion of numbers between 0 and 15. This will simplify the presentation by allowing them to use a four-bit binary number.

What success looks like: Students choose the correct conversion technique and demonstrate it in logical steps using a presentation package or other suitable software. They use one presentation page for each step in the conversion. The information will be clearly laid out and illustrated with images. Explanations will be accurate and concise.

Curriculum coverage

This chapter covers part or all of the requirements for the Computing Programme of Study (age 11–14):

↗ use at least two programming languages, one of which is textual, to solve a variety of computational problems

↗ create digital artefacts for a given audience.

This chapter also covers these main requirements for the Computing at School (CAS) Progression Pathways (for a full list of requirements met, see pages 9–10 of this handbook):

↗ understand that programming bridges the gap between algorithmic solutions and computers

↗ practical experience of a high-level textual language

↗ use a range of operators and expressions (e.g. Boolean), and apply them in the context of program control

↗ select the appropriate data types and define data types: real numbers and Boolean

↗ detect and correct syntactical errors.

Preparation

Please read the section, 'Preparing to use Python' in the introduction to this handbook (page 14) before you begin this topic. Make sure you know how students can open Python and start to create programs. When using Python, students will typically have two windows open on the screen at the same time. In one window, students write the program. The other window is the Python Shell, where the output of the program will appear.

Learning outcomes

In this chapter students will make a multiple choice quiz using the Python programming language. When students run the program they have made, the quiz will display a series of questions on the screen. The user will pick an answer, and the computer will say if the answer is right or wrong.

By completing this chapter students will be able to:

● write a program in Python
● create a program with inputs, outputs and processes
● plan a program by setting out an algorithm
● use `if... else` and a logical test to vary the output of a program
● use variables and change the value of a variable
● use relational and arithmetic operators.

Students will also develop their understanding of computer systems. They will be able to explain:

● why an interpreter is needed to run a Python program
● the meaning of 'running' a program
● how programs implement algorithms
● the main relational operators
● the main arithmetic operators.

Make a quiz

 ## Talk about...

The discussion is an activity you can do offline. You could use this activity any time to vary the pace of lessons and encourage students to reflect on their learning.

1 **Computerised tests:** Some students like tests that are run by the computer. They don't worry that much about getting the answers right. Would you prefer a test marked by your teacher or by a computer? What are the advantages and the disadvantages of each method?

   o Computerised tests are used in many subjects and may be used more in the future. Teachers often use computerised tests informally to review student learning. Some exam boards use computerised tests to deliver some qualifications. The advantages for the person giving the test are clear—marking and assessment is automatic. Automatic marking and assessment means testing is cheaper and easier. You get the results more quickly.

   o Disadvantages are the limits to the type of assessment that can be carried out. There are limitations to the multiple choice format and we cannot use computerised assessment to mark essays and reports automatically.

   o Students may like the multiple choice format because it is less stressful to be marked 'wrong' by a computer. On the other hand, they may find it frustrating and limiting when there is no single right answer.

2 **Collecting personal data:** Computers can be used to collect medical details or other information that people might feel is hard to share with a person face to face. What are the advantages and disadvantages of this?

   o This question encourages students to think about the social and personal implications of advances in technology. Computers provide an 'impersonal' way to collect data. A program can produce set responses to user input. This can include the provision of medical, legal or welfare advice. This means

standard advice can be provided at low cost to large populations. People have even reported they can find it easier to 'talk' to a computer because the computer doesn't judge them. Of course the limitations are also clear. The computer is restricted to pre-programmed responses. The computer also does not have the sensitivity or training of a human adviser.

 ## Offline activity...

The offline activity gives students a chance to do creative work without using computers. You could use this activity to introduce Python. You can also use this task if the school computers are down, or if you need to work for one lesson in a room with no computers.

In this chapter students will make a computer quiz. The quiz can be on any topic that students choose. The chapter uses a multiple choice format. Working independently, in pairs or teams, students can write suitable questions. They have to think of a question and also four answers. The answers must be reasonable, but only one can be right.

This task will give students a chance to reflect on planning the multiple choice quiz, without worrying about implementing the program code. They can develop quiz questions before the programming challenge, or alongside their programming skills.

FACT

Students may be too young to have heard of the Monty Python TV show. It is interesting to know that the people who invent programming languages also have interests outside technology. If students were able to invent a new programming language, what would they name it?

Word cloud

The Word cloud contains all the key words that have been highlighted and defined in Key words boxes throughout the lesson. The key words for this chapter are: program, information, if, else, assign a value, run, comment, prompt, machine code, interpreter, relational operator, indented, arithmetic operator, logical operator.

When they have completed this lesson students should be able to:

↗ write a program in Python

↗ create a program with inputs, outputs and processes.

More-confident students will:

↗ explore using Python to carry out simple calculations.

Overview

Students have created programs using the visual language App Inventor. In this chapter students will use a text-based language called Python. The concepts they learned in the App Inventor chapter will help them with Python.

In this lesson students will make their first use of the Python development environment, IDLE. They will produce screen output using a series of print commands. They will look at the way IDLE formats code, and use IDLE to run simple commands.

Language development

An important technical term used in this lesson is machine code. Machine code is the electronic number language that computers use. Human programmers almost never write programs in machine code. When we run a Python program, we tell the computer to convert our commands into machine code.

This chapter revisits and reinforces some terms already used.

- Students have already used the concept of a 'process' in Chapter 1, Computational thinking. This chapter revisits the concept and applies it to a computer process.

- Students have used the term 'string' in Chapter 3, Data and the CPU. This chapter revisits the term.

Before the lesson

Make sure Python is installed on all the computers that students will use. There is no need to set up special logins or any other features.

In this lesson students use the Python Shell, which lets the user enter commands one at a time. In the rest of the chapter, students will create and save a Python program in a separate window. Make sure you understand and can recognise the two windows. Remember to read the section, 'Preparing to use

Python' in the introduction to this handbook (page 14) before you begin.

To ensure that the Python Shell opens when students start up the program, you must adjust Python settings before the lesson begins. Choose Configure IDLE from the Options menu.

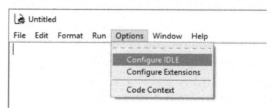

Select the General tab. At the top of the screen, select the option Open Shell Window. Selecting this option ensures that when students start Python they will see the Shell Window, matching what is explained in the Student Book.

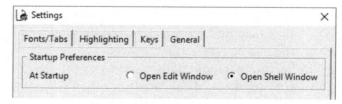

If you don't get the chance to do this, students may see the File Edit window when they start Python. This doesn't matter too much. Students can open the Shell Window themselves, from the Run menu.

The key words for this lesson are: interpreter, machine code and run. The words are highlighted when they first appear in the text. Their definitions are included in the Key words box at the end of the lesson. You may want to review these words before the lesson.

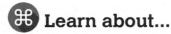 Learn about...

You will lead the first part of the lesson. Make sure students understand these ideas. You may ask them to make notes. You may use directed questioning to check understanding.

- **Machine code:** Machine code is a series of electronic numbers that the computer can read and understand. Machine code tells the computer what to do.
- **Interpreter:** We do not write commands in machine code. An interpreter translates our Python commands into machine code. The interpreter translates the commands one at a time. Some programming languages use 'compilers' instead of interpreters. A compiler translates all the commands in a program in one go.
- **Run a command:** When we run a command, we send it to the computer processor. The processor carries out the command.

In this lesson students will use the print command to produce output on the computer screen.

How to...

In the second part of the lesson student will complete an exercise under your guidance.

- **Start Python:** Take time to make sure students have started up the program correctly. Make sure they understand which of the two windows they should use.
- **Enter commands:** In this lesson students just use the print command. They see that commands must be entered with no errors (e.g. punctuation and capitalisation). If there are errors, they see an error message—just as when using App Inventor.
- **Colour:** Point out to students the colours that IDLE uses to distinguish different terms. If they enter a command wrongly, they may see the wrong colours. Demonstrate this by entering `Print` instead of `print`.
- **Print out your evidence:** You may want students to print out their work each lesson to keep a paper record. As an alternative, you may be happy just to note that students have met the requirements of the task.

Now you do it...

Students can print out any messages they choose on the computer screen. Students who are confident can pass on to the extension activity. This will give

you time to help students who are struggling to get going with Python.

What success looks like: Students use the interface and produce lines of code without syntax errors.

If you have time...

Students use the arithmetic operators + - / * to make Python carry out calculations. Students who are confident with maths can explore the effect of placing brackets in different positions in the command. For example, what is the output of each of these commands? Why is it different between the two versions?

```
print(2+3*4+1)
print((2+3)*(4+1))
```

What success looks like: Students use arithmetic operators to carry out calculations.

FACT

Encourage students to install Python on their computer at home. You may want to show them how to do this. Python is free to install and this will let them continue to code out of classroom time.

Test yourself...

FOUNDATION QUESTIONS

1 Name two different programming languages. Answer: Students are most likely to mention App Inventor and Python, which are the languages they have used. However, there are many others. If students mention a name you are uncertain of, a quick Google search will tell you if it is a programming language.

2 What is shown in green in a Python program? Answer: Strings—a series of characters in quotation marks—are shown in green.

3 Write the Python code that would print out the name of your school. Answer: The answer depends on the name of the school, but it should look similar to:
```
print("Saint Peter's Academy")
```
Note that if a string includes an apostrophe, as shown here, then the string must be enclosed in double quotation marks. In this case, we do not use single quotation marks because these look the same as an apostrophe. In other cases, either type of quotation mark may be used.

EXTENSION QUESTIONS

4 What is the job of a piece of software called an interpreter? Answer: An interpreter turns program commands that you write into machine code, which the computer understands.

5 Here are two different Python commands. What is the output on the screen following each command?

```
print(100/4)
print("100/4")
```

Answer: The output of the first command is 25. The output of the second command is 100/4. The second answer is 100/4 because the second output is in quotation marks, so it is a string not a calculation.

4.2 Create and run a program

pages 96–99

Learning outcomes

When they have completed this lesson students should be able to:

↗ write a program in Python

↗ create a program with inputs, outputs and processes.

More-confident students will:

↗ extend the program with additional lines of code, using the skills they have developed.

Overview

In this lesson students will create a Python program using print commands and comment lines. Students will save and run the program.

Students should already know how to use the Python print command, and how to recognise some of the text colours used by the IDLE development environment.

You and students should save the program to continue to work on it in Lesson 4.3.

Language development

Students will use print commands to display messages on the screen. Students will add comments to the program. Python will identify spelling errors in Python key words such as print, and will display an error message.

Python will not identify spelling errors in the character strings used in messages and comments. If students need language support, ask them to check their spellings, and note any errors.

Before the lesson

The key words for this lesson are: comment and program. The words are highlighted when they first appear in the text. Their definitions are

included in the Key words box at the end of the lesson. You may want to review these words before the lesson.

Learn about...

You will lead the first part of the lesson. Make sure students understand these ideas. You may ask them to make notes. You may use directed questioning to check understanding.

● **Program:** In Lesson 4.1 students entered single Python commands that were carried out immediately by the computer. In this lesson students make a program. A program is a series of stored commands. The commands are stored as a file. When students run the program, the interpreter works through the commands, translating each into machine code and carrying it out.

● **Comment lines:** Programmers add comments to their programs. Comments are ignored by the interpreter and are not converted into machine code. Comments are there for the human reader. Comments explain what the program does, perhaps who wrote it and when. They will show the structure of the program. Remind students to add comments to their programs.

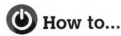 **How to...**

In the second part of the lesson students will complete an exercise under your guidance. If you have an interactive whiteboard that shows your computer screen, you can enter the program code step by step and display it to students. You could, alternatively, write the code on a display board with marker pen.

- **Enter commands as a program file:** Show students how to start a new program file (see image). A new window opens, called the edit window. Students can enter commands in the edit window to make a program with several lines of code. Unlike commands entered into the Python Shell, these lines are not carried out immediately.

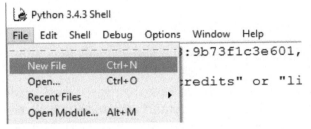

- **Add comments:** A line that starts with a # symbol is a comment. IDLE shows comments in red.
- **Save and run:** The menu bar at the top of the window lets you save and run the program.
- **Spot syntax errors:** There may be syntax errors in the program code. When you try to run the program, the interpreter will identify any errors and show an error message. You may make a deliberate mistake to demonstrate this.
- **Program output:** The program output is displayed in the Python Shell window.

Students can work at their own computers as you demonstrate how to create a program that displays text on the screen. They can copy your code and then extend it to show the question and answers they have personally developed.

 **Now you do it...**

Students' create a program that displays one question with four answers, only one of which is right.

What success looks like: Students run the program and show you the output of a question and four

answers. Give credit to students who have at least produced some display, even if it is not complete. The programming is what is important.

 If you have time...

Students extend their program to display up to ten different questions. This will give confident and able students an extended and productive activity, allowing you to support students who are struggling.

An example of an input command is:

```
input()
```

If students enter this command exactly as shown, it will pause the display until the reader presses the Enter key. This means that the reader has time to read the question before going on to the next.

Remind able students to use comments. For example, they might use comments to introduce each question and perhaps to note the right answer.

 Test yourself...

FOUNDATION QUESTIONS

1 Explain what this Python command does:
   ```
   print("\n")
   ```
   Answer: The command prints a line break, giving an empty line in the text output.

2 You have two windows open on the screen: a Python program file and the Python Shell. When you run a program, where does the output appear? Answer: The output appears in the Python Shell window.

EXTENSION QUESTIONS

3 Identify the syntax error in this line of code:
   ```
   Print("What is the right answer?")
   ```
   Answer: The word 'print' should be all in lower case.

4 What is the effect of the # symbol in Python code? Answer: To show messages explaining the program for the human reader.

Learning outcomes

When they have completed this lesson students should be able to:

↗ use variables to store values

↗ allow the user to input new values.

More-confident students will:

↗ write Python commands to change the value of a variable using arithmetic operators.

Overview

In Chapter 2, App Inventor, students learned what a variable is and how to use variables in programming. In this chapter students will work with Python variables.

In this lesson students will write commands to store the user's answer to each quiz question as a variable. They will also write commands to store a quiz score for the user. This lesson will not complete the task—the remaining lessons will add full functionality to the quiz.

Students may have made a quiz with one question, or up to ten questions. Encourage students who are ahead of the rest of the class to add more questions to make a longer quiz.

Language development

In technical language we 'assign a value to a variable'. All three words have specific technical meanings that are explained in the text.

- **Variable:** A variable is a named area of memory.
- **Value:** A value is data that may be stored in the area of memory.
- **Assign:** Assign means to put the value into the variable.

There is also an opportunity for non-technical language development. Writing good quiz questions and multiple choice answers gives students a chance to develop and display language skills.

Before the lesson

Students have to frame both questions and answers to make the quiz. If students are having difficulties with this task due to language limitations, you could provide some ready-made questions prepared in advance. Or you may take this as an opportunity for students to practise language skills. Consider

whether you need to provide extra time for students in this case.

Each piece of work in this chapter builds on the previous lesson. Work should be saved between lessons. If you have saved your program from the previous lesson, open it and be ready to continue working on it as you add functionality.

Students should also have their saved work ready for further development. If any students have not completed the previous work they must do that before continuing with this lesson. Students who are behind can catch up with the rest of the class by working from the Student Book. This advice applies to all lessons in this chapter.

The key words for this lesson are: assign a value and prompt. The words are highlighted when they first appear in the text. Their definitions are included in the Key words box at the end of the lesson. You may want to review these words before the lesson.

⌘ Learn about...

You will lead the first part of the lesson. Make sure students understand these ideas. You may ask them to make notes. You may use directed questioning to check understanding.

- **What is a variable?** A variable is a named area of storage. A variable can hold a data value such as a number. The value stored inside the variable may change.
- **Naming variables:** You should use a name that tells you what value is stored in the variable, for example, 'score'. Many Python programmers use lower-case letters only, to name variables, but this is not a firm rule.
- **Data types:** Data types are a major topic that is covered throughout the whole *Matrix* series. For now, students should be aware that Python

stores number values and text values using different methods. The quiz score is a number. The quiz answer is a single letter (stored as a text string).

 ## How to...

In the second part of the lesson students will complete an exercise under your guidance. If you have an interactive whiteboard that shows your computer screen, you can enter the program code and display it to students. You could, alternatively, write the code on a display board with marker pen.

- **Assign a value to a variable:** Use the equals sign to assign a value to a variable. For example, we can set the score to zero at the start of the quiz.

```
score = 0
```

- **Input a value to a variable:** Use the input command to let the user enter a value and store it as a variable. Add a message called a prompt to tell the user what they need to enter.

```
answer = input("Type a letter A-D: ")
```

- **Show example:** Show the program code as it should appear when completed.

 ## Now you do it...

Students add these two commands to their program. The first command will set score to zero. This command will be entered once at the top of the program. The second command will input the user's answer to a question. This command will be entered after every question in the quiz.

What success looks like: Students add to their program so that it is similar to the code in the Student Book. In this line, the value 0 is assigned to the variable score:

```
score = 0
```

In this line, user input is assigned to the variable answer:

```
answer = input("Type a letter A—D: ")
```

Note: The quiz program does not have full functionality yet. For example, there is no message

to tell users whether they get the questions right or wrong. The quiz does not keep score. The program will be extended in the rest of the chapter.

 ## If you have time...

Using the instructions in the Student Book, students add a command so the score goes up by one after each question and another command so that the final score is shown. In the rest of the chapter, students will add commands so that the score only goes up if the user gets a question right.

What success looks like: Students add this code to their program:

```
score = score + 1
print(score)
```

 ## Test yourself...

FOUNDATION QUESTIONS

1 Every variable must have a name. Explain how to choose a good name for a variable. Answer: 'The name you choose for the variable must remind you of what data you will store in that variable' or similar phrases. Good students may also mention other points: Variable names must consist of letters, numbers and the underscore character only; variable names must begin with a letter; variable names should not be too long and complicated.

2 Here is a line of Python. What is the name of the variable? What value is assigned to the variable?

```
age = 15
```

Answer: The variable is called `age`. The value 15 is stored in the variable.

EXTENSION QUESTIONS

3 Write a line of code that lets the user input a value to the variable `name`. Make sure you include a prompt to tell the user what to enter. Answer:

```
name = input("Enter your name")
```

4 Write a line of code that prints out the value stored in the variable `name`. Answer:

```
print(name)
```

Learning outcomes

When they have completed this lesson students should be able to:

↗ plan a program by setting out an algorithm

↗ use a logical test to vary the output of a program.

More-confident students will:

↗ use graphics software to produce a high quality flow chart algorithm.

Overview

In this lesson students will not do any Python coding. Instead they will plan their code. Planning a program before coding is good programming practice. In Chapter 1, Computational thinking, students learned to think about the logical structure of an algorithm. A program plan is an example of an algorithm.

This lesson includes the use of logical tests and relational operators, already covered in Chapter 2, App Inventor. Students will see how these concepts are used in a different programming context.

Language development

'Data' and 'information' are linked words. In everyday English language they are often used interchangeably. In computer science, however, data is contrasted with information. Data means raw, or unprocessed, facts and figures. Information means data that has been processed to organise or transform it in some way. Computers are used for 'information processing', that is, to turn data into information.

Before the lesson

Students will draw flowcharts. You can provide suitable paper and pens, and/or graphics software to create the chart layout.

The key word for this lesson is: information. The word is highlighted when it first appears in the text. The definition is included in the Key words box at the end of the lesson. You may want to review this word before the lesson.

⌘ Learn about...

You will lead the first part of the lesson. Make sure students understand these ideas. You may ask them to make notes. You may use directed questioning to check understanding.

- **Process:** Processing can give a transformation. A computer transforms data into information. Information is more organised and useful because it has been processed. Most programs are created to produce these kinds of results for a client.

- **Algorithm:** Students have learned about algorithms. Explain that a program plan is a type of algorithm.

- **Avoiding errors:** Syntax errors are not the only type of error. Planning before you code and testing afterwards will help you to spot other errors. Encourage students to remember that being a good programmer does not mean you never make mistakes. Being a good programmer means you work to spot errors and correct them.

⏻ How to...

In the second part of the lesson students complete an exercise under your guidance. Details of the task requirements are in the Student Book.

- **Plan the program:** Discuss and write down the input, output and processing requirements of the quiz program.

- **Use logical tests:** We want the quiz program to do different things according to whether the user gets the question right or wrong. What is the logical test we use? What actions should the computer take if the test is 'true', or if the test is 'false'?

- **Drawn an algorithm:** Draw a flow chart using the methods learned in Chapter 1, Computational thinking. The flow chart should include start, stop, input, output and decision boxes.

Now you do it...

Students draw a complete flow chart algorithm to represent a single quiz question and how the computer processes the answer.

What success looks like: The completed student work should look something like this.

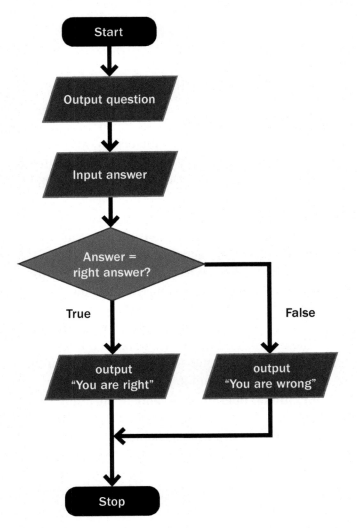

 # If you have time...

More able students can produce higher quality content. For example, they might use graphics software to produce a chart.

What success looks like: Students use suitable software to make an attractive diagram. For example, they might use Microsoft Visio, which includes a flow chart template.

 # Test yourself...

FOUNDATION QUESTIONS

1 Why is it easier to spot a syntax error than a logical error? Answer: The computer will show an error message if you make a syntax error. However, if you make a logical error, the computer will not show a message.

2 What flowchart shape is used to show a logical test? Answer: A diamond shape.

EXTENSION QUESTIONS

3 Explain the benefits a programmer gets from setting out the algorithm of a program before starting work. Answer: Students may mention all or some of these points. A fuller answer should receive extra credit. An algorithm guides programmers' work as they write the program. An algorithm helps programmers explain the program to other people. An algorithm keeps a record of what the program does. An algorithm helps to reduce errors.

4 In Chapter 2, App Inventor, you made an app which showed an ID card. What were the inputs, processes and outputs of that app? Answer: There were two inputs: click a button and type a password. The output was your name and your photo was displayed on the screen. The processing was a logical test to check if you had typed the right password. If the password was right, the outputs were displayed.

Learning outcomes

When they have completed this lesson students should be able to:

↗ use relational operators

↗ use `if... else` and a logical test to vary the output of a program.

More-confident students will:

↗ work independently, applying what they have learned.

Overview

Students have created a quiz containing one or more questions. However, at the moment the program has no additional functionality. The computer does not tell the user whether they have answered the questions correctly. In this lesson students will use an `if... else` structure with a logical test to add this feature to the quiz.

Students have already used `if` blocks, logical tests, and the relational operator 'equal to' in Chapter 2, App Inventor. Students have already planned the structure of the program in Lesson 4.4. Now they will apply these different areas of understanding.

Language development

The English words `if` and `else` are used as key words in Python. These words have similar meanings to their use in everyday speech.

- `if` : commands that follow `if` are carried out if the result of the test is 'true'
- `else` : commands that follow `else` are carried out if the result of the test is 'false'

Relational operator is a specialist technical term. Relational operator means a symbol that is used to compare two values. In Python examples are `==` and `!=`. These mean 'equal to' and 'not equal to'.

Before the lesson

The key words for this lesson are: `else`, `if`, indented and relational operator. The words are highlighted when they first appear in the text. Their definitions are included in the Key words box at the end of the lesson. You may want to review these words before the lesson.

⌘ Learn about...

You will lead the first part of the lesson. Make sure students understand these ideas. You may ask them to make notes. You may use directed questioning to check understanding.

- **Conditional structure:** A conditional structure includes a logical test. The computer chooses between different actions depending on the result of the logical test. Students have already learned to use conditional structures in Chapter 1, Computational thinking and Chapter 2, App Inventor. Revisit this learning. The use of conditional structures is a key concept in computer science. It is important that students understand it.

- **Relational operators:** Relational operators vary between different computer languages. The examples shown in this chapter are the relational operators used in Python. Write the operators for students to see, and explain their meaning. Students must note down the symbols and their meanings.

- **Comparing values:** Demonstrate how relational operators are used to create logical tests, which can be 'true' or 'false'. Students copy the examples given in the lesson, and extend the table with further examples of their own.

⏻ How to...

In the second part of the lesson students complete an exercise under your guidance. All the activities are fully explained in the Student Book. You may want to load a saved program and adapt it on screen as students watch.

- **Use `if` in Python:** Explain the structure of an `if` statement. Make sure you get all the details exactly right or there will be a syntax error. Explain how indentation is used to show the statements that belong 'inside' the conditional structure. Students add an `if` statement after question 1 of their quiz program.

- **Use `if... else` in Python:** Demonstrate how to extend the `if` structure into an `if... else` structure with two different statements. Students expand the `if` structure after question 1 into an `if... else` structure.

- **Make improvements:** Suggest ways that students could improve the output of their program.

⊕ Now you do it...

Students add an `if... else` statement to at least one question in the quiz. They then try to go on to the extension activities.

What success looks like: This is a typical example, although the right answer will vary between questions.

```
if answer == "A":
    print ("You got it right")
else:
    print ("You got it wrong")
```

⊕ If you have time...

Students extend their quiz to include multiple questions. They improve the output messages and format the quiz so that it is as discussed in the classroom.

What success looks like: Here is a typical improved example.

```
if answer == "A":
    print ("Yes, oxygen is needed for respiration. You win!")
else:
    print ("No, the answer is A (oxygen). Better luck next time")
```

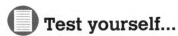 Test yourself...

The questions relate to the extract from a Python program shown on page 111 of the Student Book.

FOUNDATION QUESTIONS

1 A variable is used in this code. What is the name of the variable? Answer: The variable is called `elevenplus`.

2 What relational operator is used in this code? Answer: The relational operator `==` is used in the code.

EXTENSION QUESTIONS

3 What logical test is used in this program? What is the meaning of this logical test? Answer: The logical test is

```
elevenplus == "Y"
```

This means that the text value input from the user and stored in the variable `elevenplus` is the letter `Y`.

4 What is the output if the result of this logical test is 'false'? Answer: If the logical test is 'false' the output text is:

```
"Not old enough for this ride"
```

Learning outcomes

When they have completed this lesson students should be able to:

↗ use variables and change the value of a variable

↗ use relational and arithmetic operators.

More-confident students will:

↗ use logical operators in programming.

Overview

In this final lesson students will learn to use arithmetic operators (such as + and *) to carry out calculations. In this example they will increase the score by 1 each time the user gets a question right.

There is a longer extension activity than in previous lessons. Students who have progressed with confidence can learn an additional topic on using logical operators.

Language development

This language development advice relates to the extension activity. The logical operators and, or and not are used in this activity. These operators are used to connect logical tests together. These words have similar meanings to their use in everyday English language.

Using **and, or, not**	What it means
A and B	Both A and B are 'true'
A or B	At least one out of A and B is 'true'
not A	A is not 'true'

Before the lesson

The key words for this lesson are: arithmetic operator and logical operator. The words are highlighted when they first appear in the text. Their definitions are included in the Key words box at the end of the lesson. You may want to review these words before the lesson.

⌘ Learn about...

You will lead the first part of the lesson. Make sure students understand these ideas. You may ask them to make notes. You may use directed questioning to check understanding.

- **Assign a value:** The equals sign is used to assign a value to a variable. The key phrase to remember is:

  Variable = Value

  The name of the variable comes first, then an equals sign, then the value to assign to the variable.

- **Arithmetic operators:** The 'Value' statement can be a number value such as 0. It can also be a calculation. The computer will work out the result of the calculation and then assign the result to a variable. Calculations use arithmetic operators. Explain arithmetic operators to students and ensure they note them down.

- **Change value of a variable:** A common use of arithmetic operators is to change the value of a variable. The name of the variable appears on both sides of the equation. For example, to increase the variable **score** by one, use this command:

  `score = score + 1`

 How to...

In the second part of the lesson students will complete an activity under your guidance. You may load a saved program and continue to adapt it as students watch.

- **Increase score:** Demonstrate how to add code to the program to increase the score by 1, if the player gets the question right. Students add similar code to their own programs.

- **Output score:** Demonstrate how to output the score at the end of the quiz.

⊕ Now you do it...

Students apply the skills they have learned to create a quiz with several questions. The quiz also keeps score. If there is time, students can test the program using the test strategy learned in Chapter 2, App Inventor.

What success looks like: Ask students to demonstrate the quiz program, and make sure the program gives you the correct score. As an alternative, students can print out their finished code. The full code for one question is in the Student Book (page 113).

 ## If you have time...

Students may be able to complete this activity on their own. You may possibly have time to cover this topic in class.

- **Logical operators:** Logical operators are used to combine logical tests.
- **Using logical operators in the program:** Use logical operators to allow the program to accept upper-case **or** lower-case letters as answers (i.e both).

What success looks like: The code is given in the Student Book (page 114).

 ## Test yourself...

FOUNDATION QUESTIONS

1 What arithmetic operator is used to multiply two numbers? Answer: *

2 Write a line of code that outputs the value of a variable called `age`. Answer:

```
print(age)
```

3 Extend the code you wrote for question 2 so that the program also outputs some text explaining what the variable is. Answer:

```
print("Your age is ", age)
```

EXTENSION QUESTIONS

4 A programmer decided that if the user answered a really difficult question correctly, the score would go up by 2. Write the line of code that increases the variable `score` by 2. Answer:

```
score = score + 2
```

5 You want to check that two logical tests are BOTH true. What logical operator would you use? Answer: `and`

The test questions and assessment activities in the Student Book give you an opportunity to evaluate students' understanding. The questions are shown here with possible answers.

 ## Model answers to test questions

1 What happens when you assign a value to a variable? Answer: The student may say 'the value is stored in the variable'. A more strictly accurate statement is 'the value is stored in the memory area represented by the variable'. Either should count as a correct answer.

2 Write a line of code that assigns the value 50 to a variable called `cost`. Answer:

```
cost = 50
```

3 Write a line of code that increases the value of the variable `cost` by 5. Answer:

```
cost = cost + 5
```

4 List four relational operators and explain their meaning. Answer:

Relational operator	What it means
+	Add
-	Subtract
*	multiply
/	divide

5 How do you indicate a comment in Python? What are comments used for? Answer: Comments are indicated by the # symbol. Comments are used to add messages for the human reader. Extra credit: Comments are ignored by the computer (or by the interpreter). Comments are not converted into machine code.

6 What is the difference between data and information? Answer: Data means raw facts and figures. Information is data which has been processed. Extra credit: Processing makes data more organised and/or more useful.

7 What does software called an interpreter do? Answer: An interpreter turns Python code into machine code which the computer can understand. Extra credit: It translates into machine code one line at a time.

8 Why does a programmer plan an algorithm before beginning to write a program? Answer: There are several right answers. Reasons include: An algorithm guides programmers' work as they write the program. An algorithm helps programmers explain the program to other people. An algorithm keeps a record of what the program does. An algorithm helps to reduce errors

9 Write a logical test that gives the result 'true' if a variable `age` is greater than 18. Answer:

```
age > 18
```

10 Here is an extract from a Python program:

```
if score > 75:
    print("you have passed the test")
```

Extend this code to show a message if the score is not more than 75. Answer:

```
if score > 75:
    print("you have passed the test")
else:
    print("you have not passed the test")
```

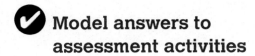

Model answers to assessment activities

Starter activity

Students have to copy the code exactly and explain it.

What success looks like: The code entered should exactly reflect what is provided in the Student Book. The student has either made no syntax errors, or has recognised and responded to error messages.

Description of the program: The purpose of this code is to assess a password entered by the user. If the text entered by the user is the word 'Enterprise' then the message 'Password is correct' is displayed.

Intermediate activity

What success looks like: Students should extend the code as shown. Answer:

```
password = input("Enter the password")
if password == "Enterprise":
      print("Password is correct")
else:
      print("Wrong password")
```

Extension activity

Activity 1: Student use a logical operator to extend the logical test. The correct code will look like this. Answer:

```
password = input("Enter the password")
if password == "Enterprise" or
password == "enterprise":
      print("Password is correct")
else:
      print("Wrong password")
```

Activity 2: Students test the program and record results. Answer: A test table for this program may look like the table shown below:

Test	Test	Test Data	Expected result	Actual result	Analysis
1	Correct password	`Enterprise`	`"Password is correct"`	`"Password is correct"`	Program works as expected
2	Alternate password—all lower case	`enterprise`	`"Password is correct"`	`"Password is correct"`	Program works as expected
3	Alternate password—all upper case	`ENTERPRISE`	`"Password is correct"`	`"Wrong password"`	Upper-case password does not work. Do we need to amend the program?
4	Incorrect password	`Voyager`	`"Wrong password"`	`"Wrong password"`	Program works as expected

Curriculum coverage

This chapter covers part or all of the requirements for the Computing Programme of Study (age 11–14):

↗ understand the hardware and software components that make up computer systems and how they communicate with each other

↗ understand a range of ways to use technology safely, respectfully, responsibly and securely

This chapter also covers these main requirements for the Computing at School (CAS) Progression Pathways (for a full list of requirements met, see pages 9–10 of this handbook):

↗ know that there is a range of operating systems and application software for the same hardware.

Preparation

To prepare for the lessons in this chapter, identify videos on the Internet, from providers such as YouTube, which illustrate some of the systems that you can't demonstrate in the classroom. For instance, Lesson 5.1 covers automatic input devices. A video of a retail checkout system featuring a barcode reader will illustrate this type of system.

Plan to use what is available in your school to provide examples of hardware and systems discussed in the chapter. For example, Lesson 5.4 discusses networks. If you have a well-developed network in your school, it will be mostly invisible to students. However, with some planning, you might be able to use this infrastructure to illustrate the lesson.

Students can search the Internet to help them complete many of the activities in this chapter. Find suitable websites that will help you guide those students who need support during a lesson.

Look at the Kidsmart website:

www.kidsmart.org.uk

The Kidsmart website supports the learning in Lessons 5.5 and 5.6.

Learning outcomes

By completing the activities in this chapter students will develop confidence and knowledge. They will be able to:

● explain the difference between a manual and an automatic input device

● describe a variety of external input, output and storage devices

● explain and give examples of system and application software

● explain the relationship between user, software and hardware

● describe different types of computer network and explain their advantages and disadvantages

● describe e-safety

● understand where to get help if you need it

● stay safe online.

Computer hardware and software

 Offline activity

Using your device

The discussion is an activity you can do offline. You could use this activity any time to vary the pace of lessons and encourage students to reflect on their learning.

The offline activity asks students to discuss their own use of computer devices and software applications. Start this activity with an open discussion about what a computer is. Many students may use a smart phone, but may not consider it to be a computer device. In fact, their smart phones are more powerful than the computers on board the Apollo spacecraft that landed on the moon. Your students can work in small groups for this activity, but should produce their own written response. Summarise the work with the whole class at the end of the session.

Word cloud

The Word cloud contains all the key words that have been highlighted and defined in Key words boxes throughout the lesson. The key words for this chapter are: input device, automatic input device, manual input device, output device, storage device, system software, operating system, application software, social network, e-safety, malware, phishing, firewall, LAN, WAN.

FACT

The introductory pages to the chapter highlight a fascinating fact about the first hard disk drive. Students discover that it would take around 100,000 early disk drives to store the same amount of data as a modern laptop. The comparative sizes of computers people used fifty years ago and those we have now could be an interesting topic for class discussion. What are the advantages and disadvantages of the relatively smaller computers that we use today?

Learning outcomes

When they have completed this lesson students should be able to:

↗ explain the difference between a manual and automatic input device

↗ describe a variety of external input devices.

More-confident students will:

↗ describe circumstances where automatic input is appropriate.

Overview

This lesson introduces input devices in a computer system. The lesson begins by defining a range of manual input devices. Students will have already used many of the manual devices described. In particular, they will be familiar with a keyboard and mouse. The lesson introduces a range of other devices including the microphone, touchscreen and camera. Students may not be as familiar with these devices.

The lesson also introduces automatic input devices, such as barcode readers. Students may have experienced barcode readers in retail stores. They may also see automatic readers used in school. For example, many library systems use automatic data input.

The lesson gives students an opportunity to build on their life experience of seeing and using some of these devices.

Before the lesson

Identify any opportunities in your school or neighbourhood that provide examples of input devices. You may also be able to find examples of input devices to show students in school.

Are there examples of automatic input devices in the school that you can demonstrate to students? You may find examples in the library where barcode readers are commonly used. Or, perhaps you have an entry system controlled by ID cards.

There are many case studies of automatic input devices in business and industrial settings. For example, barcode readers are becoming a common feature of shopping. Students might even have used one in a modern supermarket where barcode readers are now used on self-service checkouts. In industry, car assembly plants are now automated with robots doing much of the work that people used to do. Sensors track cars as they pass through a production line. Input from the sensors controls the action of robots as a car passes through the assembly line.

The key words for this lesson are: automatic input device, input device and manual input device. The words are highlighted in the text the first time they appear. Their definitions are included in the Key words box at the end of the lesson. You may want to review these words before the lesson.

⌘ Learn about...

You will lead the first part of the lesson. Make sure students understand these ideas. You may ask them to make notes. You may use directed questioning to check understanding.

- **Manual devices:** Manual devices are multi-purpose and flexible. Devices such as the mouse and keyboard can be used in any application. However, specialised input devices have been developed to perform better in particular circumstances. A games console is a good example. You can play games with a keyboard or mouse, but a special controller makes gameplay easier.

- **Automatic devices:** Automatic devices are used to make repetitive and predictable data input faster and more accurate. If data can be reduced to short numeric codes, they can be read automatically. A barcode reader in a retail outlet is a good example.

⏻ How to...

This lesson is one of the few that has no '**How to...**' section. This lesson focuses on the detail of input devices. Rather than guiding students through an exercise, you can help students understand the range of input devices and how they work, through demonstrations and videos. Here are some ideas:

1 Did you find any input devices in your school that you can demonstrate? A visualiser is a good example. You could use a visualiser to demonstrate the layout of a keyboard, for example.

2 Are there any devices in the school that have been purchased to support students with disability in the past? If so, you can set up the device and allow students to try it. If not, there are videos on YouTube that are inspiring and show what can be achieved with technology.

3 There are videos on YouTube demonstrating 3D scanners in action. A 3D scanner creates a 3D model of a real life object. They are often used alongside 3D printers. 3D scanner videos are visual and will engage students.

4 You will find many videos of barcode readers being used in retail situations. If your school library uses a barcode reader, can you arrange a demonstration of that system?

⊕ Now you do it...

The activity encourages students to consider a games console as a computing device. They are asked to identify input devices in a systematic way. If you find you have a student who has no interest in games consoles, they may consider another device. A smart phone will be a good alternative.

Encourage students to use and annotate the images they have found of their favourite console to illustrate their answer.

What success looks like: Students should identify a range of input devices that are either built into their chosen device or are peripheral add-on devices. For example, identifying a specialised controller for car or aircraft simulations would show students' understanding. They include appropriate images from their Internet research to illustrate their answer.

🌐 If you have time...

Supermarket checkouts will be familiar to most students, but these can be deceptively complex. There is a risk in this activity that students will find resources that are too technical. They need to find general demonstrations. It may be necessary to redirect students to appropriate content.

What success looks like: Students find an appropriate diagram with the main components of a checkout labelled. This includes the input devices (a scanner and keypad) and also the output devices (receipt printer and screen). Students identify the main advantages of using a barcode reader, which are speed and accuracy. Students recognise the possible errors that can arise if a barcode is attached to the wrong item or if a barcode is damaged and the data have to be input by hand.

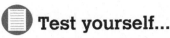 Test yourself...

FOUNDATION QUESTIONS

1 Give an example of an automatic input device. Where would it be used? Answer: A range of answers is possible:
- **Barcode readers:** Barcode readers are used in supermarkets and other retail outlets.
- **Scanners:** Document scanners are found in the home and office. People use these devices to scan documents so that the documents can be displayed on a computer. Biometric scanners are found in entry systems in buildings.
- **Sensors:** Sensors are found in buildings controlling heating or air-conditioning systems. Sensors also control security systems. They are also found in industrial settings, and in robotic and automated production lines. Sensors will track products through a production line starting and ending processes as items move along.

2 Give an example of a manual input device and explain what it does. Answer: A range of answers is possible:
- **Keyboard:** A keyboard is a multi-purpose input device that a person uses to input instructions and data to a computer. The keyboard contains letter, number and special character keys. It also has keys, such as the function keys, that control tasks (e.g. increasing the brightness of the screen).
- **Mouse:** Moving a mouse around on the surface of a desk allows the user to move a cursor around on a computer screen. Once the mouse is in the position the user wants, a click of the mouse button causes an action to take place. A mouse is called a 'point and click device'.
- Other answers may include explanations of a touchscreen, microphone and webcam.

EXTENSION QUESTIONS

3 Is an automatic input device better than a manual input device? Explain your thinking. Answer: An automatic input device is only better than a manual device where the data being collected are expected and static.

4 How could different input sensors improve your life in the future? Answer: Students may mention examples of sensors controlling household devices in response to changes in the local environment. Examples would include blinds that close as the sun moves around to shine directly onto a window. Voice control of devices may feature in answers. A TV could be told to change channels and record even when the remote control is lost, for example. Your students might mention sensors on cars that support self-driven vehicles or provide automatic braking in dangerous situations.

5.2 Identifying output and storage devices

pages 124–127

Learning outcomes

When they have completed this lesson students should be able to:

* describe a variety of output devices
* describe a variety of storage devices.

More-confident students will:

* creatively design and evaluate different input, output and storage devices.

Overview

This lesson introduces output and storage devices in a computer system. The lesson begins by defining a range of output devices. Students will already be familiar with many of the output devices described. In particular, they will be familiar with a computer screen and printer.

The lesson goes on to introduce a range of storage devices. Students will learn about storage technologies including hard disk, optical and solid state drives.

Before the lesson

Identify any opportunities that exist within your school or the neighbourhood that provide examples of output and storage devices. You may also be able to find examples of output and storage devices to show students. If you have access to a decommissioned hard disk drive (HDD), remove the casing so students can see the disk and head assembly.

There are many videos and animations available on YouTube that illustrate how a laser or ink-jet printer works. There are also demonstrations of 3D printing. These have high visual impact and could be used to discuss how printing will develop in the future. You will find some good examples on YouTube by using the search term '3D printing'. You can also use the search term 'additive manufacturing' to find some impressive of videos of 3D printing in metal. Students might be surprised to learn that some components in modern aircraft are printed.

The key words for this lesson are: output device and storage device. The words are highlighted in the text the first time they appear. Their definitions are included in the Key words box at the end of the lesson. You may want to review these words before the lesson.

⌘ Learn about...

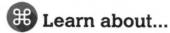

You will lead the first part of the lesson. Make sure students understand these ideas. You may ask them to make notes. You may use directed questioning to check understanding.

* **Output devices:** There are several types of output device. Each one takes digital information from the computer and converts it into a format that people can understand.
* **Printers:** Printers convert digital data into hard copy. Examples are laser and ink-jet printers.
* **Speakers:** Speakers convert digital signals into sound. Examples are internal or external speakers and headphones.
* **Monitors and projectors:** Monitors and projectors turn digital data into text, images or video that are displayed as light on a screen.
* **Games devices, tablets and phones:** These devices may use vibration to provide alerts and feedback from games. This is not mentioned in the text, but students will be aware that tablets and phones can vibrate. Students probably do not think of this as computer output.
* **Storage devices:** There are several types of storage device including hard disk, optical and solid state drives. Each type of device has advantages and disadvantages. Most computers have more than one type of storage. There are internal and external versions of all storage devices. External storage devices are portable, but these can be lost or stolen. Cloud storage is becoming more common as more users are connected to the Internet.

⏻ How to...

In the second part of the lesson students complete an exercise under your guidance. You may adapt the exercise to the circumstances in your school. This part of the lesson is best carried out in a computer room. Being in the computer room gives students the chance to explore the equipment and identify input, output and storage devices. You may be able to bring devices into the room that are not normally used there, to add to the experience. For instance, a scanner, headphones or visualiser.

 ## Now you do it...

The requirements for this activity are the same as in the 'How to...' section. The lesson will be successful if it takes place in a computer room. Depending on the equipment that is already in the room, you may need to bring in extra equipment for students to explore. Students will need access to a camera to take pictures of their chosen devices. It may be best for them to work in small groups when gathering images.

What success looks like: Students capture images of devices that closely match the devices listed. They correctly identify whether each device is an input, output or storage device and justify their answers.

 ## If you have time...

Students are free to use their imagination in this activity to create a technology system. However, they must ensure that all the elements of a technology system are in place in their design. They should include a range of input, output and storage devices. Where those devices are positioned is relevant, but the presence and suitability of devices is the most important factor.

What success looks like: Students provide a clear statement of the purpose of the system. The devices they choose to meet that requirement are appropriate and clearly identified as input, storage or output devices.

 ## Test yourself...

FOUNDATION QUESTIONS

1 Name and describe three output devices. Answer: A range of answers is possible. Printer: A printer is used to create a hard copy of an image or document on paper. Printers may produce colour or black and white output. Examples are laser printers and ink-jet printers. Speakers: Speakers take a digital signal from the computer and turn that signal into sound that people can hear. Monitor: A monitor takes a digital signal from the computer and turns that signal into images that people can see. The images are made up of dots of coloured light. Projector: A projector takes a digital signal from a computer and projects a large image onto a screen or wall.

2 What are the advantages of SSDs? Answer: Solid state drives (SSDs) are smaller and lighter than disk drives. The weight and size of a drive is an important factor in mobile devices, such as laptops and smart phones. There are no moving parts in an SSD. This makes SSDs faster than conventional hard disk drives.

EXTENSION QUESTIONS

3 What is the difference between an ink-jet printer and a laser printer? Answer: An ink-jet printer sprays dots of ink directly onto a page to create an image or text. A laser printer creates an electric image of a page on a drum using a powerful laser. The electric charge attracts toner which is transferred onto a page. A laser printer is faster than an ink-jet and cheaper at high volumes.

4 Name a piece of hardware that might be used as both an input and output device. Answer: The touchscreen is used as an input and output device. Some larger printers, or Multi Function Devices (MFDs), have both printing (output) and scanning (input) functions.

Learning outcomes

When they have completed this lesson students should be able to:

↗ explain and give examples of system software

↗ explain and give examples of application software (apps)

↗ explain the relationship between user, software and hardware.

More-confident students will:

↗ distinguish between operating system functions and the functions of hardware and application software.

Overview

In this lesson students will learn about the role of software in a computer system. They will learn to distinguish between application (apps) and system software. By the end of the lesson students will be able to name examples of both application and system software. In the activities students will consider the relationship between hardware, software and the user.

Language development

The words 'application' and 'utility' may be new to students. You could make their technical definitions clear by using an example from the home. In the home, we call services such as gas, electricity and water 'utilities'. These utilities are of little use to us unless we have 'applications' for them. A washing machine is an example of an application in the home. Without utilities, water and electricity, the washing machine cannot operate.

Before the lesson

Identify any opportunities that exist within your school to demonstrate different operating systems. If you have tablets that run iOS and tablets that run Android, make both types available for this lesson. This will give students the opportunity to contrast and compare during the lesson.

The key words for this lesson are: system software, operating system and application software (app). The words are highlighted in the text the first time they appear. Their definitions are included in the Key words box at the end of the lesson. You may want to review these words before the lesson.

⌘ Learn about...

You will lead the first part of the lesson. Make sure students understand these ideas. You may ask them to make notes. You may use directed questioning to check understanding.

● **Types of software:** Software is divided into application (apps) and system software including operating systems.

● **The role of an operating system:** The operating system manages all of the computer's hardware and software. Demonstrate what is meant by a graphical user interface.

● **Operating system examples:** Describe the common operating systems that students will encounter and the devices they run on.

● **How application software and operating system software work together:** Application software accesses the computer's hardware through the operating system.

⏻ How to...

In the second part of the lesson students complete an exercise under your guidance. You may want to prepare students through a question and answer session that reinforces their understanding of which operating system runs on a range of devices. For example, show an image of an iPhone and ask students to identify that the operating system is iOS.

⊕ Now you do it...

Students identify an application, the operating system it runs on and the device used. Some applications will run on multiple devices and operating systems. Your students should identify an appropriate combination.

What success looks like: Successful students will identify a correct combination of hardware, operating system and application software. Students may present the combination clearly in a graphical format. Students might illustrate their diagram with icons or screenshots. For example, they might include a Windows or Android icon to illustrate the operating system.

 If you have time...

This activity challenges students to identify functions that are the responsibility of the operating system. Students should not confuse the operating system's responsibilities with those of the software or the hardware. Most of the utilities in an operating system operate invisibly in the background. Most student responses will therefore focus on the graphical user interface and file system.

What success looks like: Students should provide clear examples of operating system functions. Students should present two or three meaningful examples with strong explanations.

 Test yourself...

FOUNDATION QUESTIONS

1 What is system software? Give two examples. Answer: System software manages the computer's hardware and software resources. System software includes operating systems, utility and driver software. Examples: Students will probably provide examples of operating systems such as Windows, Linux, macOS and Android. They may also include utility software or drivers. The lesson refers to drivers in a general sense, but students should explain the purpose of a driver. For example, they might provide an example of a printer driver.

2 What is application software? Give two examples. Answer: Application software is a program designed to do a specific task. For example, a word processor is used to create documents. Examples of application software: These will include word processors, spreadsheets and graphics packages. Students will probably use examples they are familiar with from home or school, such as Microsoft Excel.

EXTENSION QUESTIONS

3 Give an example of an operating system that uses a GUI. Answer: Windows, macOS and Android are examples that students will know. There are also a variety of Linux operating systems which use a GUI, such as Ubuntu or Mint.

4 What is a software program? Answer: A software program is a set of instructions that directs a computer to carry out tasks. Software gives instructions that computer hardware runs. The best responses will include a reference to categories of software programs; application and system software.

Overview

This lesson introduces computer networks. A network is defined as two or more computers connected together to share data. Local area networks (LANs) and wide area networks (WANs) are also described in the lesson. Students will learn about the advantages and disadvantages of networks. The lesson introduces the different types of network and wireless networking.

Language development

The term 'mobile phone' is used in the text. In some countries, the terms 'cell phone' or 'cellular network' may be more familiar to students.

Before the lesson

This lesson is best taught in a computer room. The computer room should provide opportunities for students to explore what networking looks like in a real-life environment. Make sure you know the location of network cabling conduits, network points and wireless access points. If there is a wall-mounted hub in the room, arrange for it to be open so that students can see the cabling. If the hub is elsewhere, arrange for students to see it so that they can recognise what a hub looks like. If it is safe, arrange for a visit to the server room, if you have one. A visit to the server room could make students understand how much cable is hidden away in your school.

Remember: Computer network rooms are potentially dangerous places. These rooms are also vulnerable to damage. Make sure you plan any activity carefully to avoid risk to students and to network equipment.

The key words for this lesson are: LAN and WAN. The words are highlighted in the text the first time they appear. Their definitions are included in the Key words box at the end of the lesson. You may want to review these words before the lesson.

⌘ Learn about...

You will lead the first part of the lesson. Make sure students understand these ideas. You may ask them to make notes. You may use directed questioning to check understanding.

- **Computer network:** A computer network is where two or more computers are connected together to share data. The two main types of computer network are local area networks (LANs) and wide area networks (WANs).

- A LAN means that each computer is connected by cables to a large, powerful computer known as a server. Students may be able to see the cables connected into sockets on the wall. If they are using laptops, they may be connected to the LAN by a wireless connection.

- A WAN is usually spread over a large area. WANs can be made by joining many local area networks together. The Internet is a WAN.

- **Advantages of networks:** With networks, it is easy to share files between computers. You can store data on a file server and back them up regularly. Having a network means computers can share printers instead of using one each, which saves money. Networks can also cut software costs, since software may be bought for a network at a cheaper price than for individual computers. A network can also help keep all computers on that network up to date.

- **Disadvantages of networks:** A network can increase costs because it needs cables, servers, switches and hubs. A human manager may be needed to maintain the network, making sure it works efficiently, which adds to costs. A network may make it easier for a virus to spread, since a network connects computers together. A network can lose more data than an individual computer if it is hacked or broken.

- **Common network types:** Bus, ring and star are common network types. In a bus network, one main cable connects all the computers. In a ring network, computers connect to each other to form a circuit or ring. In a star network, computers connect to a central hub or switch, which sends and receives the data for each computer.

 How to...

In the second part of the lesson students will complete an exercise under your guidance. Lead students through a discussion of the three types of LAN. If you have a network in your school, it will almost certainly be a star network. Your school network is a resource you can use to help students understand networks better.

1 Put together a simple plan of your school network that shows:
  - the location of the server room
  - the location of hubs (these may be in special rooms, in wall cabinets or in teaching rooms)
  - which rooms link to which hubs
  - where wireless access points are located.
2 Find out if you have a technician in the school who can spend a little time with you during this lesson. You could prepare a few questions in advance and give students a chance to ask questions.
  - How are hubs connected together?
  - How are computers connected to a hub?
  - How many devices are on the network?
  - What is involved in managing the network?
  - What would happen if a cable broke?
3 Point out network equipment in the computer room and any other available locations.
  - Can you show students the network points, network cables, hubs or switches, wireless access points?

 Now you do it...

Students should correctly identify the main elements of a network that they can see externally. These elements include network points, network cabling, wireless access points and hubs. The distinction between a hub and switch is not important for this activity. The equipment they can identify will depend on what is available for them to see within your school.

What success looks like: Students identify and name network equipment, cabling and connectors confidently. They state how a network device is connected to the network (wired or wireless).

 If you have time...

Students carry out Internet research to answer the questions in the extension activity. You may want to make sure that students have found material that is age appropriate. The content should be aimed at a suitably-simple level.

What success looks like: A successful student identifies that: mobile phones connect wirelessly to the network; phones connect to the network through local antennae; phones connect on a unique frequency; as users move around, they will connect via the nearest antenna. Students recognise a mobile phone antenna.

 Test yourself...

FOUNDATION QUESTIONS

1 Define a computer network. Answer: A computer network is where two or more computers are connected together to share data.
2 Describe three types of LAN. Answer: The Student Book covers three types of LAN. Ring: each computer is connected to the next in a circle. Bus: each computer is connected to a central cable (bus), which carries data between the computers. Star: each computer is connected directly to a hub or switch that passes data between them.

EXTENSION QUESTIONS

3 How is a LAN different from a WAN? Answer: A local area network (LAN) connects computers together in a single location, usually in a single building. A wide area network (WAN) connects networks together across large distances. The Internet is a WAN.
4 Name one advantage and one disadvantage of a star network compared to a ring network. Answer: Advantage: A star network can still work even if individual cable connections fail. Disadvantage: A star network can be more expensive because it needs extra equipment (hubs, switches, etc); a star network is more difficult to set up and needs skilled staff to manage it.

Learning outcomes

When they have completed this lesson students should be able to:

↗ describe e-safety

↗ understand where to get help if they need it.

More-confident students will:

↗ explain how to stay safe online to others.

Overview

This lesson introduces the concept of e-safety. Students will learn to use the Internet safely, including finding out how to look for help if anything they see online troubles them.

Before the lesson

Read through the lesson, paying particular attention to the section on SMART rules. Being aware of the SMART rules will help you reinforce the safety messages in the text. The Student Book directs students to the Kidsmart site:

`www.kidsmart.org.uk`

The Kidsmart site offers support to young people about staying safe online. Since the site is central to the lesson, it will be helpful if you understand its layout and content.

Make sure you are fully aware of safeguarding policy and practice in your school. You will be able to reinforce messages in the text if you can link them to accepted practice in your school. For example, the lesson states that students should always tell an adult if something has happened online that upsets them. Is there a nominated person in your school that students should report to?

The key words for this lesson are e-safety and social network. The words are highlighted in the text the first time they appear. Their definitions are included in the Key words box at the end of the lesson. You may want to review these words before the lesson.

⌘ Learn about...

You will lead the first part of the lesson. Make sure students understand these ideas. You may ask them to make notes. You may use directed questioning to check understanding.

- **Communicating online:** There are many ways students can communicate with their friends and family online, including chat rooms, instant messaging, social networks and email.
- **Chat rooms:** Websites where people get together online to type messages to one another.
- **Instant messaging:** Sending messages directly to one person or to a group, where the recipient(s) can respond immediately.
- **Social networks:** A social network is a website or other type of technology that lets people communicate using the Internet. Facebook, Instagram and Twitter are examples.
- **Email:** Using email, students can send text, images, videos and photos. Making sure they use a family or school email account, they can help protect themselves online.

⏻ How to...

In the second part of the lesson students will complete an exercise under your guidance. Students are taken through a discussion of the SMART rules on the Kidsmart website. This lesson is mostly delivering factual information. Some students might require individual support during the activities to ensure they are searching the Internet effectively. If students have already experienced online abuse or bullying they may find this topic difficult. Be prepared for different responses during the lesson and make sure that you know how to deal with any issues that may arise.

Now you do it...

Students create an advert that shows how staying SMART can help students stay safe online. They will work in pairs and use pictures to illustrate the five words represented by the acronym: Safe, Meeting, Accepting, Reliable, Tell.

What success looks like: Students produce an advert that correctly uses the five words represented in the SMART acronym. The advert include images that show the student understands the meaning of each word in the context of staying safe online. If students do not want to use pictures of themselves, they can use other images downloaded from the Internet or from another source.

 If you have time...

Students are asked to explain what online safety means.

What success looks like: Students demonstrate their understanding of online safety by listing some of the threats that exist online. The advert includes images that show students understand the meaning of each word in the context of staying safe online. They show understanding that different groups face different threats. For example, teenagers need to protect themselves from adults who may want to form inappropriate relationships. Older people may be more at risk from criminals who want to access their bank accounts.

 Test yourself...

FOUNDATION QUESTIONS

1 What does SMART stand for? Answer: SMART is a guide on how to stay safe on the Internet. The letters stand for Safe, Meeting, Accepting, Reliable, Tell.

2 Where should you go for help if you are upset by something happening online? Answer: If something upsets a student online, that student should report it to a responsible adult. A responsible adult might be a teacher or a parent, for example.

EXTENSION QUESTIONS

3 What is the difference between a chat room and a forum? Answer: A chat room is a place online where members meet to chat socially. Members will be online at the same time and chat in real time. A forum is usually set up for members to discuss a particular subject, such as a popular game or TV series. You post a comment on a forum and other members will respond to it when they happen to log on.

4 Why is there more than one form of social media? Why do people have both Facebook and Twitter accounts, instead of just one? Answer: Different social media sites are able to reach different audiences in different ways. People choose the form of social media that gets their message across to people in the most effective way.

Learning outcomes

When they have completed this lesson students should be able to:

↗ stay safe online.

More-confident students will:

↗ explain some of the specific dangers including those posed by ransomware and spyware.

Overview

This lesson takes students through some of the specific dangers from criminals using email and the Internet. Students will learn the concepts of computer viruses, phishing and spam. They will also find out the importance of recognising these threats and how firewalls can help protect data.

Language development

In English language the word 'fishing' describes catching fish by using a rod and line, or a net. In computing the word is used to describe criminals attempting to trick people into revealing personal details by sending out fake emails. The criminal, who sends out many hundreds of emails, can be said to be casting a net into the Internet hoping to catch a few unwise people. When used to mean Internet fraud, the spelling of the word is changed to 'phishing'. In English language the letters 'ph' are pronounced the same as an 'f'. Examples are pharmacy, physiotherapy and symphony.

Before the lesson

The key words for this lesson are: malware, phishing and firewall. The words are highlighted in the text the first time they appear. Their definitions are included in the Key words box at the end of the lesson. You may want to review these words before the lesson.

⌘ Learn about...

You will lead the first part of the lesson. Make sure students understand these ideas. You may ask them to make notes. You may use directed questioning to check understanding.

- **Phishing:** Phishing is when a criminal sends an email message to trick people into giving out personal information, such as bank details. The message is usually sent out by email to hundreds or thousands of people. If the criminal tricks only a few people, the phishing attempt will have been successful.

- **Spam:** Spam is an email advertising services or products that is sent to many thousands of users. The email is has not been requested by those who receive it and is usually unwelcome. Automated software is used to send out these unwelcome emails.

- **Malware:** Malware is a general term for any kind of software designed to harm computer data or steal personal information. Viruses, ransomware and spyware are all examples of malware.

- **Virus:** A computer virus is a piece of software that infects a computer in the same way that a real virus infects the human body. A computer virus can be designed to affect the performance of a computer or to damage data. Viruses can also create weaknesses in computer security making it easier to hack a computer.

- **Ransomware:** This is software that makes data and software on a computer unusable. Ransomware often encrypts data so that they cannot be read. The criminal who has sent the ransomware will demand money for a key that will unlock the data. The key makes the data usable again.

- **Spyware:** Spyware secretly installs itself on a computer then steals personal data, such as passwords and bank details.

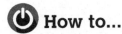 How to...

In the second part of the lesson students will complete an exercise under your guidance.

While there is no specific exercise for students to follow in this section, you can carry out one or more activities to demonstrate how to avoid malware.

- Demonstrate the antivirus software running in your school. Show students how to scan a PC using antivirus software. If you can use the antivirus software installed in your school, use that. If not, you may be able install a package on a demonstration computer and use the computer offline to perform a scan.

- Ask your school technician to demonstrate your school firewall to show how permission to use Internet sites can be blocked or permitted.

- Let students search the Internet to identify popular anti-virus software. A search for 'best antivirus software' will find lists of products. Ask them to make a note of some popular titles and explore the services that those applications provide.

- Students can search for 'worst ever computer viruses'. There are pages on the Internet that list the worst 10 viruses and describe the damage they caused. These pages will give an insight into the damage that viruses can do. YouTube offers video presentations on viruses. You could use one of these videos as part of your presentation during the lesson.

Now you do it...

The activity in this lesson reinforces students' learning about potential threats to their online safety. Students should summarise the content within the lesson.

What success looks like: Students provide answers that show they appreciate the risks of online computing. They should show that they are confident about the steps they can take to protect themselves.

 If you have time...

This extension activity challenges students to find an appropriate website that provides information on current virus threats. Students need to understand and present useful information from that site.

What success looks like: Students find and document a trusted site, possibly the site of a virus software vendor. They identify one or two current threats and describe the nature of the them.

 Test yourself...

FOUNDATION QUESTIONS

1 How can you protect yourself against a person who is phishing? Answer: Do not open or respond to any suspicious messages. Report any suspicious message to the organisation it is supposed to be sent from so that they can deal with it.

2 Explain two ways in which you can protect yourself online. Answer: A range of answers is possible. Follow the SMART guidelines and do not give out personal information; install antivirus software; make sure your operating system firewall is turned on; use different passwords for different sites—use a password manager to keep track of all passwords.

EXTENSION QUESTIONS

3 What is the difference between malware and ransomware? Answer: Malware is software that is designed to damage your computer (e.g. by installing a virus) or steal personal data. Ransomware does not steal data, but encrypts data so that they cannot be used. A criminal will try to get a ransom in exchange for a password that decrypts the data.

4 Why would a person create a virus? Answer: Some people create a virus to attempt to steal data from a computer connected to the Internet. Others create viruses that inconvenience users by damaging data or making an infected computer run slowly.

The test questions and assessment activities in the Student Book give you an opportunity to evaluate students' understanding. The questions are shown here with possible answers.

Model answers to test questions

1 What is an input device? Answer: An input device captures data from the real world and converts it to a form that the computer can store and process.

2 Give an example of a manual input device and explain what it does. Answer: Keyboard: A keyboard allows a user to input data into a computer by pressing keys. Keys can represent letters, numbers or characters. Mouse: A mouse converts movement of the mouse on a desk into movement of a pointer on screen. When the pointer is in the right position on screen pressing the mouse button will make an action take place.

3 Why might an automatic input device be better than a manual input device? Answer: An automatic input device is a more accurate and quicker method for entering certain types of data. For example, a barcode reader can capture data from barcodes on products quickly and accurately, however, the reader cannot be used for any other purpose.

4 Name and describe three output devices. Answer: Printer: A printer converts text and images stored on a computer into hard copy on a page. Speakers and headphones: Convert audio files on a computer into sound that people can hear. Screen: A screen converts text and image files into light so that people can read the screen.

5 Name a piece of hardware that is both an input and an output device. Answer: A touchscreen is an example of both an input and output device. Students will identify that the screen of a tablet can output images and text like a standard computer screen, but a tablet can also be touched to input data.

6 What does an operating system do? Answer: An operating system allows application software to talk to the computer hardware. It also provides an interface for the user to control what the computer does.

7 Describe three types of LAN. Answer: A star network joins each computer in a network to a central hub by an individual cable. A ring network joins computers together with a single cable that joins one computer to the next until a continuous circle is formed. With a bus network, computers are connected to a high speed central cable that carries data between them.

8 What does SMART stand for? Answer: Safe, meeting, accepting, reliable, tell.

9 What is phishing? Answer: Phishing is tricking someone into giving over their personal information, which might then be used for criminal activity. Phishing is an online crime usually carried out by sending emails.

10 Where should you go for help if you are upset by something happening online? Answer: Talk to an adult and let them know what has happened.

Model answers to assessment activities

Starter activity

Students will identify input, output and storage devices in the context of a desktop computer system. They will then extend that knowledge to a tablet computer, which is a more complex task since the device has all functions integrated into a single unit.

What success looks like: Students correctly identify the input output and storage devices in a desktop system. They identify the same devices in a tablet computer, even though the devices are not necessarily visible. The response to the tablet question will also need to include devices that are not present in the desktop system. For example, students might identify the touch screen as an input output device and show the position of a microphone.

Intermediate activity

Students create a cartoon that describes their interaction with technology through the course of a typical day. They will describe how they interact with a range of technology including desktop computers and mobile devices, such as phones. They will show in the cartoon what networks they use during a typical day.

What success looks like: Students create a cartoon that includes several scenes. Each scene describes their interaction with technology during a typical day. You will receive a wide range of responses from students. A successful response will include the following elements.

- Interaction with fixed, desktop equipment on a LAN: This will probably describe the student working on the school network.
- Use of mobile devices: A student might show themselves using a phone to play a game on the way to school.

- Use of technology-enabled devices: This example may focus on the home. A student who is watching TV is using computer technology, particularly if they are watching 'catch-up TV' or an entertainment system.
- The cartoon will show the networks a student connects to: A student should indicate wired, wireless and mobile networks.

Extension activity

Students will identify the five words represented in the SMART acronym: Safe, meeting, accepting, reliable, tell. They will add a sentence that explains each of the words.

What success looks like: Students demonstrate that they appreciate the importance of each of the five elements of SMART. A successful answer to this activity provides a practical action that will improve the security of the student.

Curriculum coverage

This chapter covers part or all of the requirements for the Computing Programme of Study (age 11–14):

↗ undertake creative projects that involve selecting, using, and combining multiple applications, to achieve challenging goals

↗ create digital artefacts for a given audience with attention to trustworthiness, design and usability.

This chapter also covers these main requirements for the Computing at School (CAS) Progression Pathways (for a full list of requirements met, see pages 9–10 of this handbook):

↗ evaluate the appropriateness of digital devices, Internet services and application software to achieve given goals.

Preparation

You will use several software applications during this chapter.

- **Microsoft Windows Notepad:** Notepad is a standard Windows accessory and should be available to all students working in a Windows environment. If Notepad isn't available, most simple text editors will provide the same functionality. Students will need to save files in .txt (or equivalent) format and .html. A text editor is required in Lessons 6.1, 6.2 and 6.3.

- **Microsoft Expression Web 4:** This is a freely downloadable HTML editor for use with Windows. It offers text editing and a graphical user interface (GUI). Students will carry out basic tasks, which should be supported by most HTML editors if you use an alternative. Please note, however, the illustrations are based on Microsoft Expression Web 4. This application is required in Lessons 6.5 and 6.6.

- **Picmonkey (`www.picmonkey.com`):** This is a web-based graphics application. It is one of many available on the Internet. Although Picmonkey is recommended in the text, there are no illustrative screen shots so you may choose an alternative. Make sure you can access the site and that it is not blocked by your firewall. You will need to do this before Lesson 6.6.

Learning outcomes

By completing these activities students will be able to:

- use HTML to edit or create a web page
- describe HTML

- identify basic HTML tags used in a website's source code
- explain the essential components of good web design
- sketch a wireframe design for a web page
- use images and hyperlinks on a web page
- edit a web page using a GUI and HTML editing.

Create a website

Talk about...

The discussion is an activity you can do offline. You could use this activity any time to vary the pace of lessons and encourage students to reflect on their learning.

What makes a good website?

Students can discuss this in pairs or groups.

- What are your favourite websites?
- What attracts you to each website?
- Do your favourite websites share common features?
- What do you think makes a good website?

Word cloud

The Word cloud contains all the key words that have been highlighted and defined in Key words boxes throughout the lesson. The key words for this chapter are: HTML, tag, hyperlink, navigation, wireframe, content, web browser, nesting, home page, copyright, ordered lists, unordered lists.

6.1 Starting HTML

Learning outcomes

When they have completed this lesson students should be able to:

↗ describe HTML

↗ identify basic HTML tags used in a website's source code

↗ use HTML to create the basic structure of a web page.

More-confident students will:

↗ add basic unformatted text content to an HTML page.

Overview

This lesson introduces students to basic HTML concepts. HTML is a mark up language. Students will learn how to recognise tags by viewing web page source code in a browser. The lesson covers the basic structure of a web page with the requirement to define a page head and body.

Students will use a text editor to build the basic structure of a web page using the < !DOCTYPE >, < html >, < head > and < body > tags. The lesson gives students a base from which to build a website. It introduces:

● principles of good practice in indentation

● consistent use of upper-case and lower-case letters

● how to create working text files separately from published HTML pages.

Language development

Syntax is used frequently in computing. Every computer language, including HTML, has its own syntax. Commands must obey that syntax.

In HTML a start tag must be a correctly spelled command, written inside angle brackets. For example, < head >. An end tag is the same command in brackets, but has a forward slash before it: < /head >. Every start tag must have an end tag that follows it.

English language can be clumsy if you use syntax incorrectly. An audience might struggle to make sense of what you are trying say. However, the audience for a computer language is a machine, so the consequences of bad syntax are more serious in computing. If you get the syntax wrong, the computer will reject your commands and your program will not run.

Before the lesson

Students will need a text editor for this lesson. If you are using Windows, Notepad is fine. If you are using another operating system, make sure you use an equivalent text editor. Students will need to save their work. They will build on that work in the rest of the chapter. If your school has a network, students can create a folder in their personal network area. If a network isn't available, students will need to have some other means of saving their work securely. They will be building their personal website in Lessons 6.1 to 6.3 of this chapter.

Carry out the activity yourself to identify any issues arising from the text editor you choose. For example, the lesson text tells students to save one copy of their work as a text (.txt) file and a second as an HTML (.html) file. When saving a file, Notepad has a .txt option that is accessed from the File, Save As menu. However, Notepad does not have an HTML file type available. Students need to enter the file name with the .html extension (e.g. page 1.html). The editor you choose could be different. The more issues like this that you can think through, the smoother the lesson will go.

The key words for this lesson are: HTML, tag and web browser. The words are highlighted in the text the first time they appear. Their definitions are included in the Key words box at the end of the lesson. You may want to review these words before the lesson.

⌘ Learn about...

You will lead the first part of the lesson. Make sure students understand these ideas. You may ask them to make notes. You may use directed questioning to check understanding.

- **Browser:** A browser is the software application used to view web pages. A browser translates HTML into formatted text. Make sure students are able to name three or four common browsers.
- **HTML (Hyper Text Markup Language):** HTML is used to define the format of web pages.
- **Elements and tags:** Elements are the building blocks that determine how a formatted web page will look. Tags define the characteristics of an element. For example, < p > < /p > tags define a paragraph element.
- **Web page structure:** Every web page must have a declaration, head and body. Those elements must appear in that order.

How to...

In the second part of the lesson students complete an exercise under your guidance. This section should include a practical demonstration. You could project a website onto the white board and view the source code and do the following things.

- Identify the < !DOCTYPE > , < html > , < head > and < body > tags in the source code.
- Identify the close tags, for example, < /body > .
- Explain that there are many other tags in the source code. You do not need explain what they all do but you might pick out one or two examples, such as < b > for bold text.

Now you do it...

This activity asks students to view the source code of their favourite web page, and suggests doing so with Internet Explorer. If you are using a different browser, guide students on how to view source code in that browser. Most browsers use the shortcut key CTRL-U to show source code.

Students' task is to identify the four tags they learned about in the 'How to... ' section. The source code for some students' favourite pages may be long and complicated. You can overcome this by identifying a suitable web page in advance of the lesson, then ask students to investigate that page.

Students also create a basic web page structure using a text editor. Students will need to know how to start the text editor and how to save their files. In your introduction, make sure students understand: the following.

- How to save two versions of the file they create, a .txt and an .html version.

- How to open the HTML version in a browser. The most straightforward way to open the HTML file is to double click the file icon.

What success looks like: Students recognise tags from the angle < > brackets. They identify all four of the tags introduced in the lesson within the chosen source code. Students create a blank web page structure with the four tags used in the correct order, with closing tags correctly positioned. Students save two versions of the files correctly. They also demonstrate how to open their HTML file in a browser.

If you have time...

This activity is short. Try to get all students to at least attempt the first two points in this activity.

What success looks like: Students add their name to the body of the web page they have created.

Test yourself...

FOUNDATION QUESTIONS

1 What are HTML elements used for? Answer: The elements are used to build up a web page. For example, there will be paragraph elements that contain text as well as image elements that insert pictures onto a page.

2 Name three popular web browsers. Answer: Examples include Microsoft Edge, Internet Explorer, Safari (Apple), Google Chrome and Firefox.

EXTENSION QUESTIONS

3 Name three HTML tags and explain how these are used. Answer:
  - <!DOCTYPE > : Tells the browser what language the web page is written in. The language is usually HTML.
  - <html> </html> : Tells the browser where the page to display starts and ends
  - <head> </head> : Information about the page, such as the style of text, is written between these tags. This information is not seen by the person reading the page.
  - <body> </body> : The information that is displayed on screen is written between these tags.

4 Define and explain syntax. Answer: Syntax is the set of rules that tell us how a language, such as HTML, should be used. For example, the syntax of HTML tells us tags should be written between angle brackets (<tag>).

6.2 Using tags

pages 152–155

Learning outcomes

When they have completed this lesson students should be able to:

↗ use HTML to edit or create a basic web page

↗ identify basic HTML tags used in a website's source code

↗ edit a web page using a HTML editor.

More-confident students will:

↗ change the header tag to customise the appearance of a web page.

Overview

In this lesson students will add content to the body of a web page they have created. They will also add a title to the head of the web page. They will learn that this text does not appear on their main web page, but is used to create a title for the page that is displayed in the page tab or title bar.

Language development

Indentation is used in the English language to describe a notch or hollow in the surface of an object. The word 'dent' comes from indentation. You might say, "I dented my car door."

If you indent when writing computer code, you shift blocks of code to the right in a document. As you nest commands, you indent them. Indentation makes elements of a program or HTML page easier to identify. The 'dents' you create in the program listing make it easier to read.

Before the lesson

This lesson continues from Lesson 6.1. Students will need the text editor they used in Lesson 6.1 and the files they created during that lesson. Carry out the activity yourself in advance. This will make you aware of any issues. For example, the title that students add to the head of their web page may appear differently depending on the browser version they are using. In most modern browsers the page title will appear in the tab for the page, not in the title bar.

The key word for this lesson is nesting. The word is highlighted in the text the first time it appears. The definition is included in the Key words box at the end of the lesson. You may want to review this word before the lesson.

⌘ Learn about...

You will lead the first part of the lesson. Make sure students understand these ideas. You may ask them to make notes. You may use directed questioning to check understanding.

- **Nesting:** HTML tags can be nested inside each other so that detail can be built up in layers on a web page. For example, paragraph tags are nested inside the body tags.

- **Indentation:** Indentation is setting nested elements of code a few characters to the right to make them easier to identify. Indentation is good practice and students should be familiar with it from the Chapter 4, Introducing Python. Emphasise that text indentation in HTML code does not appear on the page when it is shown in the browser window.

- **Title tag** (< title > < /title >): A title tag creates a title for a web page in the head section. The title is displayed on the title bar of the browser or on the tab of the page. The title is not displayed in the main web page.

- **Paragraph tag** (< p > < /p >): A paragraph tag is used in the body of an HTML page to define a paragraph. That is, a block of text with a space above and below it.

- **Heading tag** (< h1 > < /h1 >): A heading tag is used in the body of an HTML page to create headings in the text when it is displayed in a browser. The number that follows the 'h' defines the style and size of the heading. The number '1' is a main heading, the number '2' a secondary heading, and so on.

How to...

In the second part of the lesson students complete an exercise under your guidance. This section should include a practical demonstration. You could project onto the board, as you build up an example.

- Demonstrate the process of indenting nested elements.
- Show how to insert the title tag in the page head.
- Demonstrate how to insert the paragraph and heading tags in the page body.
- Remind students to save a .txt and .html version of the work.
- Show the completed example in a web browser. Remind students how to open a locally stored file in a browser.

If you have time, you might change a heading number to demonstrate that there are different heading types available.

 Now you do it...

Students will apply what they have learned about using paragraphs and headings to create a page about themselves. More able students can create a page that displays several paragraphs about their interests and which uses a range of headings.

What success looks like: Students create a page with a main heading and two short paragraphs, each with an appropriate heading. Each paragraph should focus on part of their life. Headings should be relevant to the paragraphs.

 If you have time...

The first part of this activity challenges students to experiment with headings beyond those introduced in the '**How to...** ' section. Students are also asked to name a set of commonly used browsers from a picture of their icons.

What success looks like: Students choose appropriate headings to reflect the content of their page. They apply headings consistently, for example, there should be a clear main heading. After that, headings should be applied to show levels of information. Students correctly identify the browsers pictured.

Test yourself...

FOUNDATION QUESTIONS

1 Why should you indent tags when nesting? Answer: Indentation makes any code easier to read. It shows that an element sits inside another. Note that indentation is not used when you nest emphasis tags around a single word. For example: `<b><i> Indentation</i></b>`.

2 What does a paragraph tag do and how would you use it? Answer: A paragraph tag groups a block of text together and creates a space above and below it, to separate it from other text. A paragraph tag `<p>` is inserted at the start of the block of text and a paragraph end tag `</p>` at the end of the text.

EXTENSION QUESTIONS

3 What is the difference between a head and a heading tag? Answer: The head tag is used to create the head of the HTML document. The head of an HTML document contains general instructions to the browser about the appearance of the web page. A heading (e.g. `<h2>`) is used in the body of a web page. A heading tag creates a bold heading that appears on a line of its own. The number after the 'h' in the tag tells the size of heading that will be shown in the browser.

4 What is the difference between a title tag and a heading tag? Answer: A title tag is used in the head of a document. A title tag creates a title, which is displayed in the browser tab for the web page. A heading tag is used to format a heading in the body of a web page. It changes what the heading looks like on screen.

6.3 Formatting text

Learning outcomes

When they have completed this lesson students should be able to:

↗ use HTML to edit a basic web page

↗ identify basic HTML tags used in a website's source code

↗ explain some of the essential components of good web design

↗ edit a web page using HTML editing.

More-confident students will:

↗ use nested tags to apply more than one format to an element of text.

Overview

In this lesson students will apply HTML tags to format the text in a web page. They will use this knowledge to add more detail to the personal web page they started in Lessons 6.1 and 6.2.

Language development

The lesson introduces students to the concept of the ordered list in HTML. The word 'order' has several meanings in English language. It can mean a command given by someone in authority. As a teacher you can order your class to be quiet, for example. Order can also be used in a less authoritative way. For instance, you can order a meal in a restaurant.

Order has a third meaning. If you order a group of objects, you organise them neatly or conveniently. You can say, "I found the item I wanted because the shop was well ordered." In this sense you are saying the shop was well organised. This is the meaning of order in the term 'ordered list'.

Please note that HTML uses American spellings. For example, it uses 'Color' instead of 'Colour' in the code.

Before the lesson

This lesson continues from Lesson 6.2. Your students will need the text editor they used in Lesson 6.1 as well as the files they created at that time. Carry out the activity yourself in advance. This will make you aware of any issues.

The key words for this lesson are: ordered lists and unordered lists. The words are highlighted in the text the first time they appear. Their definitions are included in the Key words box at the end of the lesson. You may want to review these words before the lesson.

Learn about...

You will lead the first part of the lesson. Make sure students understand these ideas. You may ask them to make notes. You may use directed questioning to check understanding.

- **The importance of design in web pages:** Web pages are a way to communicate information. The web page design is important to capture the attention of an audience. There are many factors that make a good design:
  - the sensitive use of colour and images
  - the organisation of information
  - an appropriate level of detail
  - clear language that is appropriate to the target audience.

  This is an ideal opportunity for a class or group discussion activity. The discussion could be based on a web site that you have chosen and project onto the board, or student groups could choose a favourite of their own. Students should have the chance to identify elements of design that appeal to them.

- **List types:** The distinction between ordered and unordered lists is covered briefly. There is an opportunity to do some language development. Ordered is a word with several meanings. You can also ask students to suggest examples of ordered and unordered lists. Students will have saved the work from this lesson in a new file. This applies to both .txt and .html files. They have used, but not overwritten the files from Lesson 6.2.

How to...

In the second part of the lesson students complete an exercise under your guidance.

This part of the lesson introduces students to six new tags. It also introduces the idea of nesting tags. There is a lot for them to learn in this section. You could demonstrate briefly how the new tags fit in with what students have learned already.

- **Emphasis tags:** Emphasis tags such as bold, italic and colour are usually applied to individual words rather than entire paragraphs. Emphasis tags are an ideal way to demonstrate nesting. You could use an easy task, such as, "How do we make this word bold and blue?" The tags are also close together in the text, so it is easy to demonstrate the correct order of tags and closing tags.

- **Lists:** You will have already discussed ordered and unordered lists. Demonstrate how a list and the individual items in it are tagged. This is a more complicated process for students who are used to making similar lists in word processing software.

Now you do it...

Students will apply what they have learned about emphasis tags and list tags to extend the web page they created in Lesson 6.2. They will add two or three further paragraphs of information about themselves. At least one of the paragraphs will contain a list.

What success looks like: Students demonstrate good practice using headings to show the level of information. Only two or three headings are needed. They apply emphasis and colour to the web page, focusing on key words and phrases. They will add at least one list to the web page. Students choose an appropriate list type (ordered or unordered) for the data in the list.

If you have time...

This activity challenges students to think of new sections to add to their personal web page, apart from those suggested in the lesson text. Students are asked to use nested tags to emphasise text.

What success looks like: Students have developed a page about themselves that is well organised into paragraph sections and possibly subsections. They use HTML tags to emphasise the structure of the page (heading, paragraph and list tags). Emphasis tags, such as bold and colour are used appropriately to highlight key words within paragraphs. Colour might be used in headings.

Test yourself...

FOUNDATION QUESTIONS

1 What is the tag used to make text bold? Answer: <b> and </b>

2 Write out the HTML used to make the word 'happy', bold and in italics. Answer: <b><i>happy</i></b>.

EXTENSION QUESTIONS

3 Use an example to explain the difference between an ordered and unordered list. Answer: If you give a list of instructions that must be carried out in sequence, that is an ordered list and should be numbered. A shopping list is unordered. Items are just written down as you think about them.

4 Identify three errors in this code.

```
<h1> Vital Statistics </h1>

        <h4> My Family </h5>

<p> My family is made up of <i> five people </i>. I have two sisters. My
<b> rabbit </b> is called <b> <u> <i> Comet </u> </i> </b>. <p/>

<p> My family live in an <u> apartment in the city. We enjoy going on
holiday to new places.

<p> <font color = blue> Blue </font color> is my favourite colour! </p>
```

There are more than three errors. Possible answers include:

<h4> My Family </h5> : Heading open and close tags do not match.

<b><u><i>Comet</u></i></b> : Tags closed in wrong sequence—bad practice—and <p/> should be </p> (2 errors).

<p> My family live in an <u> apartment in the city. We enjoy going on holiday to new places. : No closing tags for either <p> or <u> (2 errors). Note that the code will still work if no closing tag for <p> is used, as the next paragraph starts <p>

<font color=blue>Blue</font color>: The correct closing tag is </font>.

· ·

Learning outcomes

When they have completed this lesson students should be able to:

↗ understand the essential components of good web design

↗ sketch a wireframe design for their web page.

More-confident students will:

↗ identify suitable content for a proposed website.

Overview

In this lesson students will learn about the factors they need to consider when designing a website: purpose, audience, content and appearance.

Students will evaluate websites they have used against those factors. The lesson introduces students to wire frames as a technique for designing web pages.

Language development

The word navigation came into the English language in the 16th century. Originally, navigation meant to travel on water. Travelling on water in the 16th century was a dangerous adventure. Navigation soon took on another meaning: accurately identifying your position and planning a successful route to your destination.

Computer scientists adopted the term navigation to describe how users find their way around the huge sea of information called the Internet. When designing a website, students should imagine their audience in the middle of an ocean at night. How can students help a user identify where they are on the site? How can they help users get to the information they want to find?

Before the lesson

The 'Now you do it... ' activity for this lesson asks students to think about a website they would like to create. Their task is to make suggestions about the purpose, audience, content and appearance of the site. They are also asked to sketch a wireframe for the home page. The biggest challenge for some students will be to think of an appropriate idea for a website. Prepare one or two website suggestions before the lesson, which students can use if they cannot come up with a useable idea. As an alternative, you might create a single website idea that all students use in the activity.

The lesson text refers to a browser extension called Wirify (https://www.wirify.com/). Visit the site before the lesson and check whether the extension can be used on your school's system. If the extension might be useful in the lesson, make sure it is added to the browser bookmarks bar on each student's computer. Using Wirify is not central to the lesson. If you cannot have Wirify installed on all student computers, you could install it on your own and demonstrate it at a suitable point.

The key words for this lesson are: content, home page, navigation and wireframe. The words are highlighted in the text the first time they appear. Their definitions are included in the Key words box at the end of the lesson. You may want to review these words before the lesson.

⌘ Learn about...

You will lead the first part of the lesson. Make sure students understand these ideas. You may ask them to make notes. You may use directed questioning to check understanding. When designing a website, consider the following.

- **Purpose:** Is this site for business, information, advertising, personal use or education?
- **Audience:** Who is the site targeting? What can be done to make sure the site appeals to the target audience?
- **Content:** What information will appear on the site? What format will content take? For example, content can be text, images, audio and video.
- **Appearance:** What colours, fonts and styles will you use? Is there a house style that students need to consider?
- **Navigation:** It should be easy for the target audience to understand where they are on the site and find their way to the content.

⏻ How to...

In the second part of the lesson students complete an exercise under your guidance.

In the '**Now you do it...**' activity, students will evaluate a website against the four design criteria outlined in the lesson text: purpose, content, audience and appearance. Project a website of your choice onto the board and work through the four criteria in a question and answer session. Identify various elements of the website (navigation, content, etc.) to guide students when they come to create a wireframe. If you have chosen to install Wirify, this will be a good time to demonstrate it.

 ## Now you do it...

In the first part of the activity, students will work in groups or pairs to evaluate a website or websites they already know. The evaluation will cover:

- what the group likes about the sites and what improvements they would like to see
- a list of features that are common to all the sites they evaluate. They might list the navigation bar and search box, for example.

Encourage students to evaluate the sites against the four criteria covered in the lesson: purpose, content, audience and appearance.

Guide students on how to submit their results. A table made using word processing software is probably the most suitable tool to present findings.

What success looks like: The group submits at least one suggested improvement against each of the four criteria: purpose, content, audience and appearance. The comments need only refer to one of the sites they evaluate.

The group compile a list of common features. The list should address navigation features such as the navigation bar and search box. The group should also identify common layout elements, such as a banner, logo graphic, latest news items and so on.

The second part of the activity is carried out by each student individually. Students propose a website they would like to design. They will write a paragraph about the purpose, content, audience and appearance of the website. They will sketch a wireframe of the website home page.

What success looks like: Successful students provide a clear paragraph for each of the four design criteria. Each paragraph makes at least one relevant observation about how the proposed site can meet the criteria. Students' responses show that they appreciate the importance of the criteria for their design. The wireframe will clearly identify a banner, navigation and content elements for the proposed site's home page.

 ## If you have time...

Those students who complete the main activity may now consider the content of their proposed site. They can provide a list of possible resources that they will use in the website. They will suggest three or four sub-pages that will sit beneath the home page they proposed in the main activity.

What success looks like: The resources and page structure suggested build towards a site that is consistent with the students' work in the main activity. Students propose a range of relevant resources.

 ## Test yourself...

FOUNDATION QUESTIONS

1 What four things should you consider when sketching a wireframe? Answer: The four things to consider when designing a website are:
   o Purpose: What is the site for? Is it selling products, educating people, reporting news? Is the site clear about what it is trying to achieve?
   o Audience: Who is the site for?
   o Content: What content are you going to share with the audience?
   o Appearance: What colours, fonts and layout will you use?

2 Why is it important to consider your audience when designing a website? Answer: The site has to appeal to an audience to be successful. The audience has to feel that the creator of the website understands their concerns and needs. A site designed for teenagers will be different to a site for older people. When thinking about the audience, a designer will consider the language used on the site, the layout, the use of graphics and media and the content.

EXTENSION QUESTIONS

3 Give two advantages of using a wireframe. Answer: A wireframe is a helpful sketch of what a designer wants a site to look like. It shows where all the main elements of the site will be positioned. Those elements will include headings, navigation, text and graphics. A wireframe also helps a designer work out how the different elements of a page interact with each other.

4 What does the term 'house style' mean? Answer: House style is a set of agreed rules that are to be used on all web pages created by an organisation. The rules will say what fonts, colours, language and graphics can be used. A house style ensures that all web pages produced for the organisation have the same overall look and feel.

Learning outcomes

When they have completed this lesson students should be able to:

↗ use HTML to create a basic web page

↗ use images on a web page

↗ edit a web page using a graphical user interface (GUI) and HTML editing.

More-confident students will:

↗ change their web page to vary its look and feel, and add further images.

Overview

In this lesson student will use an HTML editor to create a simple web page that includes text and an image. This builds on the activities in Lessons 6.1 to 6.3. Students are asked to consider copyright when creating pages.

Before the lesson

Students will need an HTML editor to complete the activities in this lesson. The Student Book uses Microsoft Expression Web 4 as an example, which is available as a free download. Make sure you have requested the installation of the software on student computers in advance of this lesson. If your school uses an alternative HTML editor (e.g. Adobe Dreamweaver) then you can use that instead.

In the '**How to…**' exercise, students search for an image of a whale or dolphin to use on the web page they create. The Student Book suggests: `https://pixabay.com` as a source of copyright-free images. If you expect there might be access issues, you may suggest a different site. Alternatively, you could download suitable images before the lesson and make them available to students from a local network folder.

Students will need to do web research to find suitable text about whales and dolphins. If you are short of time, you can research and provide suitable information in a text file. It should include one or two paragraphs of descriptive text that students can use to create their own introductory paragraph. It should also include short facts that students can use to create a list.

The key word for this lesson is: copyright. The word is highlighted in the text the first time it appears. The definition is included in the Key words box at the end of the lesson. You may want to review this word before the lesson.

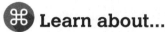 Learn about…

You will lead the first part of the lesson. Make sure students understand these ideas. You may ask them to make notes. You may use directed questioning to check understanding.

- **HTML Editor:** In Lessons 6.1 to 6.3 students used a text editor to create HTML pages. In this lesson and in Lesson 6.6 they will use an HTML editor. Explain the differences between the two. The HTML editor allows HTML to be typed in the same way that a text editor does, but has extra functions that make creating web pages easier. For example, an HTML editor has a GUI that allows elements of the web page to be positioned more easily. The editor also makes finding and correcting any errors in HTML easier.

- **Graphical User Interface (GUI):** A GUI allows a user to control a computer by using a mouse to point and click. This is faster and more intuitive for the user.

- **Copyright:** Emphasise that original work is legally protected by copyright. Students need to make sure they have permission to use resources such as pictures and music.

 How to…

In the second part of the lesson students complete an exercise under your guidance.

Students need to know how to use the HTML editor you have selected for this lesson. Students must be able to insert text and an image into a web page. When entering text, students will need to know how to format headings, change the background and font colours and emphasise text (bold, italic, etc.). When adding an image, students need to know how to locate and insert an image into the page and open the image property box to edit it. In this lesson, it is enough to know how to resize the image.

Explain to students that they need to save their files into a folder. Keeping the files together will ensure that the web browser will be able to find them.

Now you do it...

Students create a simple web page on a subject of their choice. They might choose a hobby that they are involved in. Or, they might choose a favourite football team, band or celebrity. The web page should combine text and images. It should also incorporate one or more lists.

What success looks like: Successful students create a web page that contains these elements: a main heading and consistent sub headings, text elements that are formed into paragraphs. The web page will also include appropriate emphasis, one relevant image and an appropriately formatted list. To be formatted correctly, the type of list (ordered or unordered) should be appropriate to the content. The page must open successfully in a browser. The title of the page will show in the browser tab.

If you have time...

Students who have the time will add colour, an additional image with a caption and an additional list to the web page they have created.

What success looks like: Successful students use colour appropriately to emphasise individual words or headings. Colours are chosen to enhance the content. Students take care not to create colour clash with the background colour. They use both ordered and unordered lists. They add a second picture that includes a caption.

Test yourself...

FOUNDATION QUESTIONS

1 Use an example to explain how copyright rules might be broken. Answer: Copyright rules can be broken if a piece of work is copied or distributed without the permission of the owner. For example, if a person uses a photo on a website without getting any necessary permission, he or she is illegally copying and distributing the photo. The owner is usually the person who created the photo.

2 What does GUI stand for? Answer: GUI stands for Graphical User Interface. It is a way of controlling a computer by pointing and clicking a mouse. Windows uses a GUI.

EXTENSION QUESTIONS

3 Give an example of an HTML editor and explain what an HTML editor does. Answer: Microsoft Expression Web 4 is an example of an HTML editor. A web editor allows you to create web pages without having to type in the entire HTML. It uses a GUI to create pages as well as enter HTML.

4 Why is it important to save your images and files in a main website folder? Answer: It is important so that the browser is able to find all of the files it needs to display the website correctly. Also, the files are less likely to be accidentally deleted or have their names changed by someone else.

Learning outcomes

When they have completed this lesson students should be able to:

↗ use HTML to edit and add pages to a website

↗ use images and hyperlinks on a web page

↗ edit a web page using a GUI and HTML editing.

More-confident students will:

↗ create a more complex multi-page website.

Overview

In this lesson students learn how to use online tools to edit images for their web pages. They also learn how to use hyperlinks to navigate within a website.

Before the lesson

Students will continue to use Microsoft Expression Web 4 to build on the web page development work that they completed in Lesson 6.5. If you have chosen a different HTML editor, check the 'How to... ' section of the Student Book to see if there are any tasks that cannot be done. In particular, check the section on adding an interactive button on page 170. Adding an interactive button is the function that is most likely to be different in an alternative HTML editor.

In the lesson, students are instructed to use an online graphics package to edit an image. The site suggested is Picmonkey (`www.picmonkey.com`). Make sure you know how to use the online image editor, so you can support students. You may choose a different editor. There may be an editor available on the school system that you and students have used before. There are also other online tools such as Photoshop Express Editor (`http://www.photoshop.com/tools?wf=editor`). The advantage of an online tool is that students can use it at home, if they are connected at home.

The key word for this lesson is: hyperlink. The word is highlighted in the text the first time it appears. The definition is included in the Key words box at the end of the lesson. You may want to review this word before the lesson.

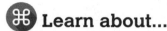 ## Learn about...

You will lead the first part of the lesson. Make sure students understand these ideas. You may ask them to make notes. You may use directed questioning to check understanding.

● **Hyperlinks:** These are attached to text or images in a web document. A hyperlink contains the address of another web page or location. Clicking a hyperlink opens the location in the browser window. Hyperlinks are used to navigate the World Wide Web.

How to...

In the second part of the lesson students complete an exercise under your guidance. These are the three skills students need to complete the learning activity.

● Add a new page to a website.

● Create hyperlinks to navigate between the pages of a website.

● Edit an image to be included in a website.

You may want to give a short demonstration to ensure students know how to add a new page and create links between two pages. You can also demonstrate how to load an image into Picmonkey (or your alternative). Demonstrate where some useful editing tools can be found in the Picmonkey menu and save the result.

Students can practise these three new skills on the site they created in Lesson 6.5.

Now you do it...

This activity asks to students to carry out two tasks: create a second web page and then evaluate their website.

In the first part, students will create a second web page related to the one they created in Lesson 6.5. The page created in Lesson 6.5 will be the home page and the page create in this lesson is a sub-page. Students will create links between the home page and the sub-page. They will also add an image to the sub-page that has been edited in a graphics package.

What success looks like: Successful students create a new page that contains text and a graphic edited in a graphics package. If questioned, students can describe the changes resulting from the edit and show the original image for comparison. They create a link with an appropriate name on the home page and this should successfully link to the new sub-page. The sub-page should contain a button that is a hyperlink back to the home page. That button should be clear and positioned appropriately.

In the second part of the activity, students will test and evaluate their website. They ask themselves seven questions. Their response to the last question will reveal the extent to which they have performed a meaningful evaluation. "If you had more time, what would you do to improve the website?" You can discuss this with students informally or ask for a written answer to the question.

What success looks like: Students identify two or more issues that they would like to address if they had more time. Their responses will relate to one of the evaluation questions they have been asked to consider in the learning activity. Their answer states the issues and outlines realistic actions that directly address each one.

 ## If you have time...

Students who have the time, will add more pages to their site to create a more complete website. The evaluation should address the entire site they have built.

What success looks like: Successful students assess their website using the same criteria as those in the '**Now you do it...** ' activity. Students only need to have edited one graphic. They should appropriately name all additional pages and links. They should maintain the logical structure of the site as they add new pages.

 # Test yourself...

FOUNDATION QUESTIONS

1 What is an interactive button and how is it used? Answer: An interactive button is an image that has a hyperlink attached to it. Clicking the image opens a new page. Interactive buttons usually use graphics that look like the buttons on a real device, such as a remote control. Sometimes buttons will be animated to make them look more interesting. Examples of interactive buttons used on web pages are the home, menu and help buttons.

2 What is a screen reader? Answer: A screen reader is a software application that reads text on screen and outputs it as audio. It is used by visually impaired people who cannot read text on the computer screen.

EXTENSION QUESTIONS

3 What is the difference between a website and a web page? Answer: A web page is a set of related information displayed as a single screen. The information on a web page can include text, images, sound and video elements. A website is a collection of related web pages.

4 Why is it important to add accessibility properties to an image? Answer: Accessibility properties allow people with disabilities to read web pages. Accessibility properties attached to images are text based. This means that a screen reader can describe an image to a visually impaired person.

The test questions and assessment activities in the Student Book give you an opportunity to evaluate students' understanding. The questions are shown here with possible answers.

Model answers to test questions

1 What is HTML and what does it stand for? Answer: Hyper Text Markup Language is a language consisting of tags. The tags are used to create documents that can be distributed over the Internet and displayed in a browser.

2 Identify and name the tags used in this example. Answer: The tags in the example are:

< !DOCTYPE >   Defines the document type

< html >   Defines an HTML document

< body >   Defines the document's body

< h1 > and < h2 > Defines a heading

< p >   Defines a paragraph

3 What is nesting? Answer: Placing one tag inside another. Nesting allows us to add more detail to a HTML page or one of its elements.

4 Give an example of how you would nest the word 'Communication' using the tags for bold and italics? Answer: < b > < i > Communication < /i > < /b >

5 Why do web designers use wireframes? Answer: Wireframes allow designers to see what a page will look like without having to think about the actual content of the page. Designers can use wireframes to plan how the elements of a web page fit together.

6 What is copyright? Answer: Copyright gives legal protection to the creator of a piece of writing, music, art or photography. Works cannot be copied without the permission of the creator.

7 Why is it useful to have a home page? Answer: The home page is the starting point for all websites. The home page tells us what a website is about. If you get lost in a website, you can return to the home page and know where you are.

8 What should you think about when evaluating a website? Answer: Purpose, audience, content and appearance. Students may give answers that are more specific, but they should all relate one of these four criteria. They might also add these two valid questions: "Does it work?" and "How can I improve it?"

9 Here is some example text: Using headings in HTML

How would you use HTML tags to define this text as a level 3 heading? Answer: < h3 > Using headings in HTML < /h3 >

10 How does alternative text attached to an image help visually impaired people? Answer: Alternative text is used so that an image can be described to a visually impaired person. The text can be read out by a screen reader. A screen reader is a device that turns the text on a page into audio.

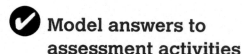 Model answers to assessment activities

Starter activity

Students will use the HTML editor to create a basic web page to a direct specification. They will make one alteration to the HTML code provided before saving the page.

What success looks like: Students use the text editing functions in an HTML editor to create a web page. The HTML is indented appropriately and easily readable. They have made the required change correctly and saved the file successfully. The web page opens successfully in a web browser and the text appears as expected.

Intermediate activity

Students will open the file they created in the Starter activity. Students will add three key facts about tags to the page and use formatting tags to add emphasis to their text. They will used nested tags on at least one occasion.

What success looks like: Students successfully locate and open the correct file. Three key facts will be added under the Tags heading of the page. Each key fact will be defined as a paragraph or as an element in a list. The key facts should be relevant and accurate. They should express the student's understanding of the content in this chapter.

Students use at least three types of emphasis with bold, italic and colour favoured over underlining, which can be mistaken for a link. At least one example of emphasis uses nested tags. The words or phrases students choose to be emphasised are be appropriate. The file is saved correctly and displays as expected in a web browser.

Extension activity

Students create a second page called Interesting facts. They will create a hyperlink from My First Page to the Interesting facts page. Students will add a list of interesting facts to the page, with each one formatted as a paragraph. They will identify their top three interesting facts and format them as an ordered list.

What success looks like: Students successfully locate and open the correct file. They add at least three interesting facts to the page. Each fact is defined as a paragraph or unordered list item. The student identifies their three favourite facts in an ordered list. The facts added to the page are relevant to the chapter content and accurate. Give extra credit to students who include facts that are not in the text, but arise from the student's own research.

Students who add a heading to the Interesting facts page, add a subheading for 'My favourite facts' and add a link back to the home page, should be given extra credit. These are not specifically requested in the activity, but add to the appearance and navigation.